CARLOS

CARLOS

RICHARD BECHT

To Mum and Dad for all your support and letting me do what I love... my way.

To Jo, I know you don't think I see everything you do for me but believe me I do!

To Payton, I look forward to you reading this one day, but don't grow up too fast my little man.

I love you all.

Cheers
Los

CONTENTS

ISBN 1-877252-15-8

Published in 2004 by Celebrity Books
Private Box 302 750
North Harbour, Auckland
New Zealand

Cover design, book design and production by Dexter Fry
Printed in China through Bookbuilders, Hong Kong

Celebrity Books is the imprint of The Celebrity Book Company Limited.
160 Bush Road
Albany, North Shore City
New Zealand

The photographs used in this book are supplied by Fotopress and the Spencer family collection except;
p1, p220/221 © Nestle Purina Petcare; p4, p39, p48, p58 Mike Walker; p42/43 McRobie
Photographics; p46 The Evening Post; p230, 232 Woman's Day/Sally Tagg.

ACKNOWLEDGEMENTS

This book would not have been possible without help and input from the following people:

Wikitoria Spencer for her persistence in collecting every article and photo about me and collating them into scrapbooks; Graham Spencer for letting me slip out the window to play league, knowing that rugby was where my passion and future lay; Jodene Williams for all her tireless work and encouragement; David Jones for initiating the book and seeing it through to its completion; Richard Becht for squeezing the information out of me; and Bill Honeybone for taking on the task.

I would also like to say cheers to everyone else for their hand in this book. It's been a nostalgic trip for me and a most enjoyable one.

CARLOS SPENCER
June 2004

Between pre-season training requirements, Super 12 matches and overseas trips, Carlos wedged in countless hours of interviewing. It's always a privilege talking to professional sports people about their existence and translating their thoughts into book form.

Gaps needed to be filled in and there was no shortage of assistance in that regard from David Jones (DOJ), whose recall was invaluable, while Jodene also had ample helpful information and advice. Greg Dyer also provided important insights into the business side of Carlos' life.

Thanks to Bill Honeybone from Celebrity Books for the chance to work on the project.

Various publications and newspapers were used as information sources, most notably a number of editions of the Rugby Almanack of New Zealand.

Finally, thanks to the photographers – especially Ross Land – whose images adorn this book.

RICHARD BECHT
June 2004

CHAPTER 1

Moko Ink

ANYONE HEADING WEST along Great North Road in Auckland will know one of the suburbs along the way. It's Grey Lynn and, just before a downhill run towards Western Springs Stadium, the road passes through an assortment of shops. One of them stands out as something of a house of pain, and it's not a dental surgery.

I had reason to be there just days out from Christmas Day 2003, at a time when the Rugby World Cup was already just a memory for me. It was something I didn't want to spend - even waste – time thinking about anymore, something I got out of my system a few weeks earlier, very soon after the event actually.

Other people were still banging on about it, of course. They were quite entitled to. Everyone has a different approach to everything, but once the World Cup had finished rugby was no longer the No 1 priority for me for the next few weeks.

So, my visit to Grey Lynn on December 19 had nothing to do with the game that's dominated my life but everything to do with me. It was a deeply personal issue, something I live with every day.

The focal point for me was a studio bearing the name Moko Ink. Get the picture now? Tattooing, of course. It was there I had a date to have some more work done on my body. Funnily enough – and I had no idea this would be the case – it was the same day the New Zealand Rugby Union was due to make its announcement about the All Black coach.

I'd stayed right out of that and, to be honest, it wasn't even on my mind when I walked into the studio. Having a new tattoo completely occupied me. Only

A lasting reminder (left) of money well spent at Moko Ink. I couldn't be happier with it.

when I was reminded about the coaching decision later that day did I give it any thought.

There I was redesigning part of my body at the same time John Mitchell was learning he would no longer be the All Black coach and that Graham Henry had the job instead. I hadn't been following the developments at all in the preceding weeks – anything but rugby, please – but the announcement briefly interrupted that plan.

I felt sorry for Mitch. I believed he deserved another shot and yet I wasn't at all unhappy about Ted being the new coach. How could I be? He'd wanted the job for years, he deserved to have it and he's such a great coach. He's proved that wherever he has been by and large, so I was really happy for him and for his wife Raewyn and their family.

I honestly wasn't too fussed about the coaching issue, though, because I'm one of those guys who'll just get on with it whoever has the job. So I'm sitting on the pickets I know but I mean it when I say I would have been happy with either of them.

Besides, on this day of all days I had something far more pressing and important on my mind. I had all these drawings on my arm which soon enough – and not without pain – would be transformed into a permanent piece of body art.

I've always had a thing about tattoos. I like them.

I had one done on the upper part of my left arm when I was a Waiopehu College fifth former in Levin, the equivalent of what's called Year 11 these days, if I'm not wrong. It was 1992, the same year I made my debut for Horowhenua, and I was 16 as I remember it. Along with a couple of mates, we drove to Palmerston North to check out a tattoo shop and, after looking around, I saw a design on the wall that I decided I wanted. It was one showing a tiger and a bit of sun, just something I thought would look good. It must have taken around three hours or so to do – and it bloody hurt, too – but I walked out with what I wanted. I thought I was cool.

I hadn't told Mum and Dad what I was up to. Instead I just came home that night and showed them what I'd done. Mum wasn't too bad about it. She's fairly relaxed about things and just said: "Oh, no." No great drama, though.

Dad was a bit different. "What the **** have you done that for?"

But by then he also knew it was too late. The damage had been done. There was no big lecture or anything like that but his reaction was what I would have expected.

Let's face it, tattoos used to carry a bit of baggage a few years back. Guys in the navy would have them as well as gang members, of course. You'd see them on blokes who looked fairly mean. That's how I read it. Tattoos weren't considered a good look back then and not many of my other mates at school had them, prob-

With my first tattoo on show at age 16 I thought I was cool.

ably because of what they meant.

Looking mean wasn't the reason why I wanted a tattoo, though, or why I've wanted more since. I just liked them and had always been interested in them. Growing up I was attracted to things that were different from what others had or did. I don't recall seeing tattoos on someone else that I wanted but I know I was fascinated looking at them on people and in books. I was set on having one myself and never regretted the choice I made when I went to that shop in Palmerston. I also had my right ear pierced around that time, which probably wasn't quite so unusual.

That first tattoo set me back something like $60 which was a reasonable amount of dosh back then. I used to work for the old man as a drain layer in the holidays to earn a bit of extra of money. As far as I was concerned, I'd put some of it to

I love what my tattoos mean as well as the look of them.

good use with that tattoo and I wasn't about to stop there either.

The following season I was in Greymouth with Horowhenua for a third division national championship match against West Coast and, just for the hell of it, I went along with my brother Fabian and one of the other players to have some tattoos done. Fabian went for one on his shoulder while I had a gravestone tattooed on my left forearm below the big one I'd had done in Palmerston North. That one took no more than an hour at the most. I couldn't tell you why I chose that design. There was no special significance about it and later, when I moved to Auckland, I had an eagle and some bats added. It was a bit rough really.

I think Mum and Dad understood the type of person I had become or was becoming when I started going the body art way. A bit different would probably be the best description. I gather that's the way a lot of people see me as well, although my friends in Canterbury would probably come up with another expression.

The business about the image I seem to have is one I can't really get my head around. A lot of it stems from living in Auckland, of course. But when I arrived in the big city I was a shy kid from Levin and nothing much has changed 10 years later. There's still a lot of my home town in me. I can be cheeky and I like to have fun but there's a difference between what I am on the field and what I am off it. My partner Jodene will tell you that. She reckons I never stop talking when I'm playing but when I'm not she says I hardly say anything. Ah, well. That's me I guess.

Especially in group situations with people I don't know so well, I'm still as shy as I was when I first left Levin. I think a lot of people see it as arrogance when they can't talk to me or when I don't talk to them. In fact, it's shyness.

I love the way Canterbury people have me sorted out. It's not too hard to work out that they hate my guts but they're great. They see me as arrogant because of the way I play, I suppose, and they have more against me because of the rivalry they believe exists between Andrew Mehrtens and me. I'm sure they don't like the way I look or even walk either, usually going on that I strut around on the field. Hell, it must be my "nua" walk, the one I've grown up with. That's the way we used to walk in Horowhenua. Sorry to say, it's not a city walk.

The fact is, on the field I like to express myself and have fun and maybe people don't like it if I smile too much or look like I'm enjoying myself. Others throughout the country feel the same way, too. They just show it in a different way, though, especially in Dunedin where the students provide real humour.

On the other side, I appreciate there are actually people who seem to like what I do. That's how it is and I wouldn't want people to be any other way. It's all good fun.

Opinions formed come through in all sorts of ways, even in comments made by former internationals like ex-Wallaby Sam Scott-Young before we played Australia in our 2003 World Cup semifinal: "That snooty little guy with the tattoos, niggle him, smash him in defence, mess up his hair...."

See, there you go – the hair and the tattoos. They're the things some people take special notice of and I'll admit they're two features I spend a bit of time on. Whether it's a Mohawk or another do, the hair cops a bit of attention. But the tattoos mean the most to me, especially the major ones I've had done over the last two years or so, one on the lower part of my left arm and the most recent one on my right arm, just a bit below the shoulder and coming down towards my elbow.

That's where Moko Ink in Grey Lynn comes into it and, most of all, the man with all the skills for the job, the man who has a business card listing his name as simply Inia III. Otherwise known as Inia Taylor, he's of Ngati Raukawa descent and is credited with doing much to revive ta moko (tattooing), achieving huge profile through the amazing work he did on the make-up side in the box office hit movie *Once Were Warriors*.

My All Blacks, Blues and Auckland team-mate Kees Meeuws is a decent advertisement for the studio with what he's had done to large areas of his body so I had a word to him about tattoos. He told me all about Inia, prompting me to make a trip to Grey Lynn after the Super 12 season and before the Air New Zealand NPC in 2002.

Now, *Once Were Warriors* was one thing, but I wasn't thinking in terms of Jake the Muss when I first met Inia. What was most important at first was the tattoo on my left arm. I wanted to cover up the gravestone, eagle and bats but I also wanted to have a design that was nice as well.

What we discovered was that there were links between Inia's family and mine from around the Otaki and Levin areas. My grandfather on Mum's side and his grandmother's sister were best mates so we had a closer connection than we had realised.

We talked and then Inia started drawing possible designs on my arm. We'd like something, change our minds, rub a bit out, try something else and we kept going like that until, through a process of elimination, we had a plan I liked. The biggest problem was coming up with something suitable to cover up the old tattoo. Rather than have a basic tattoo as such, we also wanted one with extra meaning from my Maori side. What I like about the Maori designs is that they look really good. They're striking.

After drawing all morning, Inia explains it better than I can: "At the time, Carlos' career was at a low point. He was having contract problems and it looked like he might even be going overseas. I suggested I get rid of the piece on his forearm. He didn't realise it could be covered up but I thought we could do quite a successful job of that.

"So, we used the koru in the tattoo to symbolise constant growth and constant change, and the prayer within that is the fact the koru is always obtaining a higher

Kees (Meeuws), taking a dip with Ma'a (Nonu) in 2003, provided the inspiration for me to visit Moko Ink.

state when it's growing within that forest. There's also a hawk's feather running right through the middle of it, which symbolises foresight. In Maori tradition, any weapon a chief uses will have a hawk's feather tied to it. The reason for that is that everyone lives by the decision made by that chief and (how he uses) that weapon for a long time.

"I realised that what Carlos was dealing with at the time would have repercussions for a whole lot of people, including himself. That was why the hawk's feather was significant. By using it like this, it provides the overview a hawk has, in the way a hawk hovers over a paddock looking around.

"Also included is the mango pare, the symbol for the hammerhead shark, which is all about standing your ground, strength, determination and balance, if you like strength in adversity. The other element is shark's teeth, which indicate strength and back-up, or protection and faith."

So, that's what Inia had in mind as he went to work on the final design. To say it stings just a little bit would be a lie. There are times when it hurts like hell but for four hours or so I put up with it. After a while, your skin gets a bit numb and you don't really feel much at all.

It wasn't all over and done with in a day either. I had to go back later so Inia could put some white in the design to make the imagery stand out more, to polish it up basically. At $600, it was worth every cent. I love what Inia achieved. I'm really proud of it and Jodene thinks it looks great, too.

I'm not sure I feel anything too spiritual from my tattoos as such although, with my Maori heritage, the Maori aspects, the stories the tattoos tell, mean a lot to me. While I'm proud of my Maori background, I regard myself first and foremost as a New Zealander. Not only do I love what my tattoos mean but I really love the look of them as well.

So just before Christmas 2003 I was back seeing Inia asking him to go to work on my right arm, to balance things up I suppose. I also had a fairly specific idea of what I wanted this time, three lines coming down from my shoulder and through my forearm. I definitely wanted to have it further up my arm but at some stage I might join it up and continue it further down the arm, definitely something connected with our first child.

The way Inia tells it, the second tattoo continues the shark's tooth pattern: "It was a lot to do with the shoulder problem Carlos had during the year. It serves to strengthen or fortify the shoulder and it really works. You think about it... when you get a tattoo a whole lot of white cells rush up to an area they haven't previously been given a signal to go to. It's like getting the body's healing mechanisms to concentrate on an area and that's what this tattoo was doing to Carlos' shoulder. Basically it's an extension of the tattoo on the left arm, similar in meaning but totally different in design. I think that second piece is stunning."

I couldn't agree more. Kees has had a good look and he thinks the two I've had have come up really well, too. He's a bit of an expert on them now although the other boys don't worry that much about them.

I certainly had a lot of reaction at the Rugby World Cup about the one on my left arm because it's so visible when I'm playing. Some people even remember me by my tattoo, as I discovered in Las Vegas of all places.

I was there for a week after the World Cup for Adrian Cashmore's stag-do, along with some of the boys including Charlie Riechelmann and Filo Tiatia. We were having a drink and an English guy came over to talk to me. He wasn't sure who I was but he said he recognised the tattoo before saying: "You're the Australian captain – George Gregan!"

A lot of people, especially English folk, are intrigued by the tattoos and ask me where I had them done. The day I had the second one, an English bloke walked

That tattoo (right) served two purposes, one providing me with artwork I'm proud of while at the same time covering up a dodgy tattoo I had when I was younger.

There it is again . . . I struck a lot of interest in my tattoo during Rugby World Cup year in 2003.

in to Moko Ink waiting there all day to have a tattoo done; same thing with a Swedish guy. They both wanted a Maori design. They've really caught on, maybe because Robbie Williams had a Maori-styled tattoo done.

Once Were Warriors generated a lot of interest in moko and so did the 1999 Rugby World Cup when a massive poster was draped on the side of a building in London, showing a Maori with a striking moko (it happened to be Bay of Plenty prop Warwick Morehu).

Inia has strong views on the value of people like Kees and me having pieces put on our bodies. "I think it's very good if Maori can see other Maori who've been successful, like Carlos and Kees, identifying themselves as Maori," he says. "That's really inspiring that they can do that. It also makes them a lot more accessible. What I like is that within Maori there are so many amazing individuals, there's no such thing as a typical Maori. That's what you see here. The tattoos give an individual interpretation of that person and it's really put Carlos aside from everyone else. I know after that first tattoo, it really rocked him."

Not wrong. People can say what they like but "that snooty little guy with the tattoos" couldn't be happier. I might be able to put rugby events – like World Cup losses – out of my mind fairly quickly, but I can't escape my personal body markings.

CHAPTER 2

The Place I Call Home

I'M A BIG CITY TYPE THESE DAYS but I'll always be a small-town boy at heart. Nothing can or will change that. I know people see me in a different way and reckon I'm just one of those Aucklanders now, and in many respects I am. After more than 10 years away from home, I have settled into life in the big smoke – but underneath it all the country boy is still there.

Not that Levin is strictly what you'd call a little place in the country. It's a good-sized, if fairly regular, New Zealand provincial town with a population of around 20,000, the main centre of the Horowhenua region or province in a part of the country where farming and market gardening are the main industries. It also stands out because it's on State Highway No 1 and on the main trunk railway line. It's this part of New Zealand that has always been home for me.

To set the scene here, my mother's name is Queenie but she's known as Wiki (as in Wikitoria), if you can understand that. There's nothing like that with Dad – his name is Graham – while the family is completed with my brother Fabian, who's almost four years older than me.

As you might have guessed from her name, Mum provides the Maori side of the family. She's from Dannevirke, north of Palmerston North, where my grandparents Myra and Bill Hetariki still live. While they're both Maori, Maori traditions weren't big in our family, not the way I remember it. No one I can recall actually spoke the language but there was one thing I'll never forget – the Maori feeds we used to have. We'd find any excuse to have a hangi for family gatherings and special occasions. So we had a flavour of my Maori side and certainly today one thing I'm conscious of is trying to pronounce Maori words properly. I think that's important.

An early photo of the Spencer family . . . Mum and Dad with Fabian and the centre of attention, curls and all.

Dad has spent his life around Levin, working for a long time in the drain-laying business with his brother, my uncle David. My Nan, Jean, lived in Levin for years and used to babysit Fabian and me. She shifted to Christchurch but passed away last year while my grandfather died quite a few years ago.

One talking point surrounding my brother and I has always been the names Mum and Dad gave us. There's been a lot of speculation about them over the years but there's no special secret about them at all. There's no Spanish connection or anything like that behind me being named Carlos. The way Mum tells it, mine was simply a name that appealed to them and Fabian was a singer's name way back when, which Mum and Dad liked. No family traditions or anything like that.

What did run in the family was sport. Most kids with ability usually have sport in their bloodlines and we certainly did. Dad had a rugby background playing for the Levin Wanderers club and Horowhenua while Mum's sporting ties were in netball and softball. So it surprised no one – least of all our parents – that Fabian (born November 21, 1971) and I (October 14, 1975) should develop a huge appetite for anything competitive and connected with sport.

The curls have gone but there's a hint cheeky Carlos is developing.

As for school, well, I can tell you the names of the ones I went to – Taitoko School, Levin Intermediate and Waiopehu College – but I couldn't tell you an awful lot about what went on in the classroom while I was there. Schoolwork was never one of my great strengths at all. It was, in fact, a real weakness because I went there to eat lunch, play bull-rush, touch rugby and go to phys ed classes! In saying that, I did enjoy English, social studies and science but I was never too fussed about passing School Certificate or anything like that. I was too sporty for that.

Along the way I had a form teacher who once famously told me: "You'll never get paid for playing sport!" Back in those days, there was never a thought there would be money in rugby but things kind of changed, as that teacher has no doubt discovered.

If I was to sum up my childhood I'd say I loved every minute of it, it was just awesome and I had an absolute ball throughout. I wouldn't be the person I am today if I hadn't grown up the way I was able to in Levin. It was such a good way of life, that much better because we didn't have everything handed to us on a plate. We had to work for it. What I also recall is the fantastic bunch of guys I grew up with; they were brilliant to hang around with and we always had a good time.

Dad could be fairly tough when he wanted to be, but there was nothing wrong with that. Together with Mum, he provided Fabian and me with strong values. Mum was just Mum. I could get away with murder with her. She could pack a mood sometimes but we had huge respect for her and we'd do our best to ensure

No wonder that bag looks so big – it's me heading off for my first day at school.

she was always happy. If we ever wanted something, we'd bypass Dad and butter up Mum instead. Wagging school? Not a problem. We knew Mum would write a note to the school for us. That's how she is. She's lovely.

I have the most vivid memories of all those years growing up in our family home in Heather Street, although Mum and Dad have shifted from there now. Fabian and I were very close, always playing together, a lot of touch one-on-one out on the street. Of course, we'd have our brotherly spats every now and then but nothing too serious.

To me, ours was what you'd call a typical upbringing in a fairly typical middle-class New Zealand neighbourhood. There were always lots of kids around to play with, and to play up with as well. We'd be into all sorts of things as young guys, playing cricket outside or we'd be off to a park nearby playing softball. Television wasn't a big deal for me and we certainly didn't have anything like PlayStation and XBox that today's kids apparently can't do without. We didn't even have a video game. Our fun was playing outside in the backyard. I'm told two boys can be a handful for parents but not the two of us. Fabian and I were never like that. As Mum and Dad discovered, we were perfect kids really. I know they'd agree.

They both worked – Mum as a sewing machinist – and they always provided what we needed in every way. With our sport, whether it was BMX, rugby or softball, they'd make sure we had good gear. It was a fantastic family home with heaps of support from our parents no matter what we wanted to do. That was never truer than when we both had a real passion for BMX racing. We did heaps of it and won loads of trophies, starting really young and continuing to compete until the age of 14 or 15. We had a track in Levin and most of our weekends were spent travelling as a family to various competitions around the North Island.

For a while it was probably the most important thing going for us. It was more a summer thing so we'd have rugby in winter and then BMX in our other sporting season. We'd always be cleaning our bikes, working on them and looking after them. They were our pride and joy; that whole BMX deal was such a brilliant part of my life.

Whether the passion had anything to do with me liking motorbikes, I'm not so sure. All I recall is that I always loved bikes and I used to like watching them and hearing them tear around town. There was something that attracted me to them. We had a couple of gangs – which, I will say, didn't interest me in the slightest – and we'd see these Harleys around town, which made me think to myself: "Gee, they're cool. They're awesome. I'm going to get one of those one day."

It took me a while to realise that dream but around five years or so ago I bought my first Harley. And, no, that wasn't a problem for Mum and Dad; they weren't worried about me thinking along the lines of owning a bike.

It wasn't just bikes either. Speed, noise and big machines were generally a real passion. I was into hot rods as well and I was really big on trucks. Loved them. I want to own a monster truck one day just as a bit of a toy, maybe a Big Mack Ultra-Liner or something like that.

All the time, though, rugby was there. When I was young, around five, the scene would be Playford Park in Levin. Bare feet. Saturday morning rugby. The ground freezing cold. Isn't that just about every kid's memory of starting in rugby? It was just like that for me.

I don't know exactly when it kicked in, but from a fairly early age I liked to try things on the field – I was always the one running with the ball, stepping and throwing the ball around. It just came to me. It was the way I enjoyed doing

There was a time (above) when softball meant as much to me as rugby, maybe even more for a while.

Right: The softball bug, courtesy of Mum's involvement, struck really early for a long-haired young Carlos.

An angelic-looking school kid . . . at that time BMX racing probably meant more to me than anything else really.

things and still do. I suppose I'd have to say I was always cheeky on the field, even when I was young, although I have no idea where that streak came from.

I didn't mind the idea at all of the forwards doing all the dirty work as long as I could find a way of getting my hands on the ball as much as possible. My story certainly isn't one of an All Black who, as a kid, started out as a tight forward and became a first five-eighth; there've also been plenty of stories of All Black forwards who were backs originally. With me it was a case of once a first five, always a first five. There was a little bit of second five in there along the way and later on I also had a taste of fullback but there haven't been too many times in my life when I haven't been at first five for every team I've played for.

That included the representative teams I was in from an early stage, making it into various Horowhenua age group sides including the Horowhenua Primary Schools team in 1988, the union's under-14 side the next year and also the under-16s.

Around the same time, I became more and more involved in and passionate about softball in summer, especially after my BMX days. I'd played a lot of T-ball earlier on and moved on to softball, as much through Mum's background in the sport as anything. Mainly a short stop but also a back-up pitcher, I loved the game and made the New Zealand under-16 team in both 1990 and 1991. I knew the Tangaroa family well. They were from our part of the country and New Zealand pitcher Chubb Tangaroa's father coached our side at one stage.

As a batter I wasn't too bad. I hit a few home runs here and there but I didn't stick with it long enough to play at the senior national tournament. The furthest I went was under-16 level before giving it away to concentrate on rugby. It was just too difficult to play both but I really enjoyed softball and there was a time when I probably leant more towards it than I did rugby. While I wanted to keep pursuing it, I think it was Dad who advised me there was only one direction to

These were early rugby days for father and son, with Dad (far right) as one of our coaches and me (second left, middle row) in the same team.

go and it wasn't softball.

So, it was rugby. I had four years in the Waiopehu College First XV – first making it in 1990 – and we had a damned good team. They were unforgettable days, too, some of the best times I can remember.

We played in the Manawatu competition where we'd come up against tough sides like Hato Paora College, Palmerston North Boys' High School and Feilding Agricultural High School. We also played Horowhenua College regularly and plenty of others as well while another major moment was our involvement in the World Schools' First XV Rugby Championship in Whakatane in 1992. We finished fourth in that, losing to New Plymouth Boys' High School in the semi-finals – they ended up winning it – and we were then beaten by St Stephen's College in the play-off for third and fourth.

There was a crew of us who used to hang out in our college days, the Hirini boys, Warren and Danny, the Fifita boys, Mario and Daniel, and Brendon McDonald. We'd get together after every First XV game and have a couple of quiet beers! Little sneaky ones.

Rugby at that age was simply about enjoyment. I was beginning to realise I

There were only so many things for a young kid from Levin to do so skateboarding and BMX racing took up a fair amount of my time.

might have a future in the game but right at that time I wasn't mapping out what lay ahead. I just loved every game I played. I was fully involved as well because, apart from playing first five, I also did the goalkicking for Waiopehu College as well as other teams I played in. I wouldn't say I took the goalkicking really seriously, though, because our motivation was always to score tries, especially with the talent we had in our backline.

The way I played rugby then is the approach I still have. That's where and when I probably learned all my tricks and also through playing touch. I was allowed to play that way in that Waiopehu College team, to play it the way I saw it I guess and I loved that. That's the way we grew up. We had so many players who played their rugby like that, relying on flair to get us there. We mightn't have had much choice because I don't think anyone could kick a ball to save themselves in those days.

We weren't reckless the way we played but we weren't afraid to try moves from all over the field. We were a cheeky bunch, too, causing some big conflicts whenever we played Hato Paora. As a Maori boarding school, all the pupils would be out doing their haka and trying to intimidate us so our reaction was to mix it on the field.

I guess if I'd come up through the tried and true system at a school like Auckland Grammar School, Christchurch Boys' High School or one of the other big rugby powers, a coach there probably would have tried to rein me in and play a lower-risk style of game. That's why it was such a blessing that I was brought up in Levin where I could try things, have a go and not be too scared about the consequences. I also had to grow up quickly as a player because I soon found myself playing among much older people at such a young age.

While rugby was the passion, the other rugby code had a place as well, although it required a bit of sneaky stuff on my part. Basically I played rugby union for the school on Saturdays then on Sundays it would be rugby league. I'd throw my football boots out my bedroom window, tell Mum and Dad I was off to catch up with my mates, pick up my boots and that afternoon we'd be playing league for the Foxton Rebels in the Manawatu club competition. One of the guys was Nathan Picchi, who also played for the Waiopehu College First XV, but later stuck with league. It was that time of life when you just wanted to play as much sport as you could and rugby league provided another chance. I enjoyed it, too, although I was always going to stay with the 15-man game.

Away from rugby, I wasn't a rebel cruising around on Friday nights. We didn't have cars then and had no idea what boy racers were in those days. Our go was more the space invader parlours that were all the rage then. Hell, we were all on our BMX bikes then with skateboarding being another outlet. We'd meet every Friday night and at weekends and skate through town, finding a ramp or

Do I have a clue what I'm doing with that guitar? Probably not, I'd say.

building one somewhere. We were even able to build a mini half pipe inside one spacie parlour, which was pretty good.

We stayed out of trouble, too. I was caught smoking at school once but was let off and that's about the worst thing I can remember doing, or the worst I want to remember! No, I honestly stayed out of strife. I kept smoking for a while, though, because so many kids at school were doing it but I gave up fairly soon after leaving school.

Smoking generally leads on to the subject of girls I guess, but I wasn't too out front about that sort of thing. As I said, I was very much a shy boy then and I still am now. I was the sort who would stay back behind everyone else. The girls would have to come and get me.

I was far more confident once I had my boots on and was out on a rugby field. By the age of 15 or 16 I appreciated I was a fairly decent player and my thoughts were never about staying in Levin. Well before my shift to Auckland, my ambition was to move to Wellington to see whether I could make something of myself in rugby there. I was a bit of a chance to go to Otago, too. I flew down to have a look around and have a meeting with rugby people at the time I was looking to further my career.

It was Dad who was always steering me in a certain direction. He was the one coming up with the advice on what I should be considering. He was a critic, my best/worst critic. He'd always be telling me I should be doing this, or doing that, even when I was a young kid. He tended to be the sort of Dad who would say: "What the hell did you do that for?" He was a believer in doing the basics where my way of playing the game was quite a bit different. He liked the idea of playing the percentages more.

My game was more built around running and passing then, backing up, doubling round. I didn't have so much then in the way of chip kicks, grubbers and definitely no banana kick. That was years off. I was more into keeping the ball in hand and doing something with it.

Because I've been willing to try things, I've had a lot of embarrassing moments but I wouldn't have it any other way. They happened back then and they happen now but I've never been worried if something of that type doesn't come off. I don't expect things to fail but I do accept they will sometimes. You don't know what's going to happen until you try something and I'd hate to be the sort of player who wouldn't try something because he was worried it wouldn't work. That would defeat the purpose of playing to me. The things I tried to do with the ball in my younger years all came naturally. I didn't really practise them. I'd also work on new tricks whether I was experimenting with passes or kicks. Today I get more frustrated at training when something doesn't come off than I do in a game. Obviously I'm annoyed when I make an error in a match but the thought's always there that the biggest risk is not to take one. I can see it's not an approach a lot of players are prepared to take and I find that a real shame.

Funnily enough Fabian, who was out of school by the time I began playing for the Waiopehu College First XV, was completely different in his approach. He was always more the hard yards sort of player, taking it up the guts and not so much a ball-playing No 8, but he did his job and did it well.

As a youngster, I wasn't one to watch players as such either, not in that star-struck sort of way. The only player I recall being a big fan of was Bernie Fraser, probably because he used to score so many tries and I liked that. Bernie's Corner at Athletic Park and all that meant something to me. He was exciting.

As far as first fives went, I always took notice of Grant Fox for his goalkicking but I didn't get into the hero-worship stuff. I didn't have posters of rugby players over my bedroom walls. Definitely not. My room was full of truck posters instead. That was what I liked most. A good mate of mine was keen on trucks as well. He had lots of books on them and our A4 folders were full of pictures of trucks. I had a ride in a few big trucks, too. Loved them. I liked the look of them.

Mind you, it became obvious to me that liking trucks didn't offer me any future prospects, where I came to appreciate rugby gave me a huge chance. If I wasn't totally sure about that when I was 15, I certainly knew differently at age 16. My rugby world was about to open in a very definite way.

CHAPTER 3

Sweet Sixteen

I LOVED PLAYING RUGBY with my mates at school, being among guys of a similar age who I had a lot in common with and had become used to. It's the way most rugby careers play out, to be honest. Depending on talent and what selectors think, the usual progression for a player aiming for the top is age group representative teams, your school's First XV, the New Zealand Secondary Schools team, senior club rugby, New Zealand Colts and then representative rugby (or something similar to that).

My career path started regularly enough at the very outset but then veered right off course all too soon. If one way of growing up quickly is to be taken out of your comfort zone, then I found out how true that is when I was sweet 16. From that moment on, nothing was too normal anymore.

The reason could be found in Scotty Huston, who came on board as Horowhenua's new coach in 1992. The union was stuck in the third division of what was then called the National Mutual Championship – now the Air New Zealand National Provincial Championship (NPC) – and that humble status has only occasionally changed through the years.

Scotty didn't restrict himself to just bringing a new broom in. He wheeled in an industrial-strength vacuum cleaner to turn the place upside down as he went searching for new players. He brought in plenty of them that year, including a 16-year-old Waiopehu College fifth former by the name of Spencer. It wasn't entirely straightforward, though.

One moment I was a spotty-faced 16-year-old (left) playing for his school, the next I was playing senior representative rugby.

Think on the age for a moment – 16, and I wouldn't turn 17 until almost the end of that season. It was young. I didn't consider it at all back then. When you're that age, part of you or even a lot of you thinks you're bullet-proof. Without saying it out loud, you can't wait to have a shot at the older guys.

But there was no argument that going straight into the Horowhenua representative team out of college was fairly dramatic. The way I remember it, Scotty – whose son Carl was also in the Waiopehu College First XV – approached Dad about it, asking whether I wanted to play for the senior Horowhenua representative team. The old man wasn't that keen. I think he believed I was too young to be tried at that level.

To be playing with grown men at 16 was a big jump. Put it this way, long-time winger Don Laursen was still in the team then and he was 34, more than twice my age with more than 120 games for the union behind him. Some others were up there in the age stakes as well like prop Kere Akuhata and winger Jim Barker, both of whom were well past their 30th birthdays.

I went for it, though. Whatever Dad had to say probably went through one ear and then out the other. What do I remember about coming into the team being just a schoolboy? I don't think I was that bad about it really. I was helped because some of the guys were mates, I'd met a few others through Fabian and some were family friends.

It was still difficult, though, because I was shy and found it awkward to come out and say things being that young. How does someone that young start calling moves and telling older players what to do? He struggles, of course, and yet I was treated well. The guys looked after me. Naturally the older guys gave me a bit of stick, just having some fun as more experienced players do when new faces come into a side.

The early Spencer style playing for Horowhenua when still a schoolboy.

Don't ask me to relate any specific details of my first match or even my first season at that level. All I know after checking it out is that my first appearance was on May 16, 1992, coming on as a replacement and scoring a try in a 15-25 loss to Canterbury Country. The truth? I don't remember a thing about it. That's how it is with me with much of my career. I'm not one of those guys with a photographic memory. I'm flat out trying to remember most things that happened yesterday let alone 10 or 12 years ago.

Obviously Winfield Cup rugby league jerseys were in fashion when the Waiopehu College First XV posed for this photo.

With one of my Waiopehu College team-mates Nathan Picchi, who went on to play a lot of rugby league.

I didn't realise this until recently either, but my introduction to rugby at this level also created a bit of confusion over my date of birth. I was given two different birthdays. In my two seasons with Horowhenua, my date of birth was recorded as June 14, 1975 in the Rugby Almanack of New Zealand both times; my birth certificate confirms I'm actually four months younger than that date would suggest and ultimately my shift north coincided with a uniform birthday.

In all, I made just six appearances for Horowhenua in my first season. I had a good time, too, scoring a few tries – five of them – and doing some of the goal-kicking but I had to fit in other commitments with Waiopehu College and, later in the season, I was also selected in the New Zealand Secondary Schools team. Making that side in 1992 and again in 1993 was a huge deal for me as well as

Waiopehu College and Horowhenua rugby generally. There was some unreal talent in the teams, too. So often the traditional rugby schools would dominate teams like that. But me from Waiopheu College?

"Where's Waiopehu College?"

"It's in Levin."

"Where's Levin?"

It was that sort of thing. Actually there were quite a few lesser-known schools that supplied players to the team in those two years I was involved. I'm thinking of Jeff Wilson (Cargill High School), Chresten Davis (Morrinsville College), Christian Cullen (Kapiti College), Carl Hoeft (Te Aroha College) and Anton Oliver (Marlborough Boys' High School). All of us became All Blacks from what might have been regarded as small beginnings. And Waiopehu College actually had two players in the New Zealand team in 1993, prop Daniel Harper joining me as well.

I guess it means someone was watching me – and obviously playing for Horowhenua had to help – but of all those players I came across in the national team, there was one guy who took some getting used to. I had first come across him at the New Zealand Secondary Schools sevens tournament in Auckland, a bloke who was just so massive we couldn't believe our eyes, or keep our eyes off him – Jonah Lomu, of course.

I don't remember too much about that tournament other than him. Looking at the size of him, seeing the damage he could do and watching him with the ball in hand was incredible. You'd want him in your team rather than against you, that's for sure. Just to observe him and the way he lifted his legs in full flight was something to behold.

He was just so massive among snotty-nosed schoolboys like the rest of us. He played off the back of the scrum then and every time he had the ball he'd basically break at least a couple of tackles and usually quite a few more. He'd run half the length of the field to score tries a lot of the time. He wouldn't have been too used to being tackled then because he usually just ran through or over the top of everyone in his way. I can only say again, he was massive. I can't recall ever seeing anyone that big at that age – and that quick as well, because he was really quick then.

I suppose it's reasonable to wonder what might have happened if he'd been able to stay at No 8. He had the size and strength for the job but you'd have to wonder whether he would have lasted. You'd imagine the work rate required would have been beyond him in the long term but he was some player at that age. I was

Following pages: A team photo with a real difference of the 1993 New Zealand Secondary Schools side. Holding the ball in the front row is captain Anton Oliver and that's me two further along to his left. Up in the back row Royce Willis, Chresten Davis and Jonah Lomu are all standing together.

just glad we were in the same team when we were both picked for the New Zealand schools team.

We had other special players around at that time in that age range, too. Jeff Wilson was a little bit older but I was still in the same team as him with both the New Zealand Secondary Schools in 1992 and the New Zealand Colts in 1993. He was obviously highly talented then and the same was clearly true of Cully (Christian Cullen). When I think of Christian, I think of playing against him when I was at Waiopehu College and he was at Kapiti College just down the road a bit. We were also in Horowhenua age group representative teams together and what was immediately obvious about him was his unbelievable pace. Cully always was an out and out runner, just gliding around the field, but we never got to play together for the Horowhenua senior representative team; he came into it the year I'd gone to Auckland.

Put Lomu, Wilson and Cullen together and, from a young age, I was incredibly lucky to be playing alongside three truly special performers.

My most vivid recollections of all the rugby I played at school age were being in that team in 1992 and repeating the experience in 1993. In the first year, we started our campaign against Irish Schools in New Plymouth, a match we just won but a match that doesn't register with me as much as the coach did. He was Clive Williams from Southland Boys' High School and he made us tackle tyres while

What about that hair style?

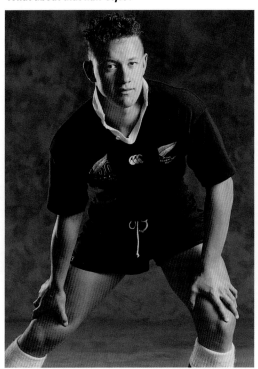

the forwards had this pole they had to go under and, if they didn't get it right, they'd hit their heads on the pole or bar. For some reason, that has stuck with me. He was a hard man.

But the most memorable aspect in 1992 was the fact selection handed me my first trip away. After meeting Irish Schools we headed to Australia for three matches culminating in us beating Australian Schools 31-8. Taking in Melbourne, Canberra and Sydney was fairly eye-opening for a boy from Levin. I think we might just have had a look at a few peep shows, too, which were probably even more eye-opening!

Also in that 1992 side were Jeremy Stanley, Daryl Gibson, Todd Miller, Isitolo Maka and Royce Willis. They all became All Blacks while we also had Trevor Leota, who went on to play for Manu Samoa.

Through going straight from school into the Horowhenua side, I really missed out on a club career in Levin, which was a pity; you couldn't do everything, though. If a lot was happening around me in 1992, even more was in store in 1993. It would be my last year at school before I left as a third-year fifth former. You read it right, third-year fifth former. I don't mind admitting it at all. It was just a fact of my life and it's never bothered me. Why should it?

Quite a few of the Waiopehu College team from that era went on to play for Horowhenua at some stage after finishing school but in 1993 three of us were all picked in the side while we were still schoolboys – winger Nopera Stewart, Daniel (Harper) and me. Nopera and I were lucky enough to play in the biggest game of our lives at that stage, a match that will always stand as a career highlight for everyone in that Horowhenua side.

What made it even better for Mum and Dad – and Fabian and I – was that we were both in the Horowhenua squad in 1993 and shared the magic of a very special day in early April, one when Fabian was making his debut.

Since 1985, Auckland had owned the Ranfurly Shield. They'd had it so long they just about deserved to keep it. They also had a great policy about taking the shield on tour, regularly defending it on the road and they were at it again by bringing shield rugby to Levin. A few days later they defended it again against Buller in Westport.

The anticipation surrounding our encounter with the great Auckland side was bigger than anything anyone had known around Levin. We had quite a build-up for the game, too. The Auckland Rugby Union sent the log down early so we could use it to promote the match. We actually took it on a bit of a tour around the union the week before, visiting schools in the whole region to let everyone see what all the fuss was about.

I was over the moon the game was in Levin. After all, I was only 17 and had the chance to play against a side including Grant Fox, Va'aiga Tuigamala, Eroni Clarke, Olo Brown, Craig Dowd and the All Black captain himself Sean Fitzpatrick. And my brother was going to be there with me as well. On top of that, Dad was the team's manager. How good was that?

I must have been nervous as hell, even the dreadlocks I had then must have been shaking, but it was an unbelievable experience that afternoon. I was lucky to have the ball in hand a bit and I managed to do a couple of things as well. I remember scoring one try myself, backing up a Craig Yorston break, and I was also involved in a try scored by my Waiopehu College team-mate Nopera (Stewart). He went something like 60 metres for that one.

We were never ever going to be the slightest chance in the game. That's never

the point of games like this. Ask any of the boys who played that day and just the chance to line up against so many good players meant everything to them. All a side like ours could do was go out and have a shot, to see what we could do, and no one could say we failed after our effort. The score was fairly decisive – Lee Stensness scored four tries himself in an 80-17 scoreline – but we lapped up every minute of the match. It was as big as anything seen at Levin Park Domain.

I seem to recall I had a bit of a spat with Foxy, too. It was a little tussle and afterwards I shook hands with him and apologised. He said: "No, don't apologise." Knowing me, being a cheeky young bloke, I probably set out to deliberately do something to him, a cheap shot.

I can't say how much of a thrill that day was for us. I've played all sorts of matches for the All Blacks, the Blues and Auckland but that game will always be one of my highlights, certainly the biggest moment I had with Horowhenua.

There was a more important event ahead for the union later in the season but, before that, I had to get my mind around a couple of other commitments. Initially there was my selection in the New Zealand Colts (under-21) for the first time, a side I made the next two years as well. It meant leaving the Horowhenua team but the guys blew me over when they all chipped in and gave me a lump of cash as I headed off. That was just a brilliant gesture from them.

Now I was still a 17-year-old among a lot of players who were already 21. I guess the stand-outs in the team were Jeff (Wilson), Andrew Mehrtens, Justin Marshall, Taine Randell, Mark Hammett, Mark Mayerhofler, and Adrian Cashmore. They were the players who went on to become All Blacks.

It was just a two-match tour with matches against Thames Valley and the Australian under-21s, for me a non-playing learning experience only when Peter Thorburn and Sid Going were the coaching staff.

Also slotting in around appearances for Horowhenua were two matches for the New Zealand Secondary Schools, both of them memorable for one very big reason – Lomu again.

We played England Schools in Dunedin first and flogged them 51-5 but there was one try above all that stood out, one when Jonah smashed his way through several of the poor Pommie boys on his way to scoring an incredible long-range try. A few weeks later he picked up two tries when we also smashed Australian Schools 32-7 in Rotorua. If rugby people hadn't guessed already, it was more obvious than ever that the big bloke was going to be really big on the world rugby scene.

That match against Australian Schools ensured a hectic end to what would be

I was still 17, beer in hand and Horowhenua had just beaten Wanganui to win the National Provincial Championship's third division final.

In my strip for the 1992 New Zealand Secondary Schools team.

my last season with Horowhenua. In just a matter of days I went from playing for the New Zealand Secondary Schools in Rotorua and the next back home in Levin teaming up with the boys as we beat Mid Canterbury 30-22 to reach the third division final.

That pitted us against neighbours Wanganui six days later, the home ground advantage being theirs. For us, though, this was a second chance to escape from the third division. The previous season Horowhenua had been denied, losing the final in the last seconds to Nelson Bays. There were several survivors from that defeat but for Fabian and me it was a new experience playing in a decider like this, a winner-take-all contest.

In his second season, Scotty Huston had shown he was a good operator at this level. He was certainly a decent coach for me to have in my first exposure to provincial rugby but now everything hung on this encounter at Spriggens Park.

The match was one of those grinds but we won it 15-9 and the result was all that counted, nothing else. I'd missed a few shots at goal; nobody cared about that, not when Horowhenua had gained promotion to the second division. Dad was spraying bubbles all over us in the dressing room but there was one disappointment for us. Fabian didn't see the match through after he popped his shoulder and had to be taken to hospital.

Still, I'd rounded off some year. I'd played all but two of Horowhenua's matches during the season and had the special thrill of being able to play alongside my brother all year. That had to be pretty cool and it was.

But it turned out I'd played my 18th and last game for my home union. My rugby future lay elsewhere. It's a fact of rugby life in New Zealand that any player with ambition – and I certainly had that by then – has to move to a bigger centre to develop his game. Always there are people around looking for future talent throughout the country. Obviously I think it's great when players are found in less likely areas such as Horowhenua. It's encouraging to know we have a chance no matter where we come from but at some stage the call must be made to move on, sad as it is for the union that's developed a player in the first place.

While I would be leaving home, Fabian went on to play more than 40 times for the union before injury slowed him down. My time at that level with Horowhenua was much briefer but so much of who I am as a person and what I am as a player can be traced back to what happened in Levin. I never forget that.

CHAPTER 4

Los(t) in the city

THE WHEELS BEGAN TO TURN for a move to Auckland months before I arrived in 1994. The seeds were, in fact, found in the Ranfurly Shield challenge Horowhenua had against Auckland in April, 1993. Otago was one possibility for a move but I wasn't that keen after looking around Dunedin one day. In many ways, Wellington might have been the most logical of all. It wouldn't have taken me that far away from home but there was never any contact with anyone from the capital.

In the end Ponsonby came knocking. If that hadn't happened I don't know what might have panned out. Maybe I would have headed to Wellington to find out what was available down there or I could have stayed another year at home I guess. A season in the second division wouldn't have been too bad but I really knew I needed to move to further myself.

Ponsonby had it all sorted, though. They had accommodation arranged and, after a few weeks, a job as well with a printing company called PDQ Print. They were one of Ponsonby's sponsors so obviously that worked in well for me. I did some packing, driving around to pick things up and had some money coming in – but the company was also flexible with my hours to fit around rugby needs. In many ways this was my first job and, apart from rugby, my only real job. The only other work I had really done was some drain-laying with Dad and my uncle.

While I was being well looked after, the first few months were still very difficult for me. I was homesick, I didn't really know anyone in Auckland and I didn't know my way around the city either. I could recall being in Auckland only twice before, once in my BMX days and then with the New Zealand Colts the previous year when we were trashed 31-8 by the Australian Under-21s. The time we were up

Here's a rare sight . . . playing club rugby for Ponsonby with Postie (Craig Innes), after he'd returned from his rugby league career.

for a BMX meeting, the old man got lost, taking a wrong turning and ending up in the city somewhere when we were meant to be over on the North Shore. I knew how he felt.

Auckland was just so big. I couldn't get over it when I arrived permanently in early 1994. One of the reasons I didn't work immediately was to give me a bit of time to look around so I could get my bearings and get settled in.

I didn't find Auckland unfriendly as some people might imagine. Not at all. It was just the size of it hit me and I didn't know where I was going most of the time. All my friends and family were back home so I didn't have anyone else I was close to that I could lean on I guess.

The rugby side of it worked out fine with Ponsonby and then with the Auckland squad but I know I kept Telecom pleased ringing home so much. Apart from my family, I had a girlfriend back in Levin. She didn't come up at first but ended up moving to Auckland as well, although not until I'd been there for the best part of six months. That made a big difference, especially once we were able to move into a flat of our own.

Overcoming the unfamiliarity of the city took a while. When I finally had it beaten, then I began to feel really comfortable. Being a homeboy from Levin, the transition to Auckland was just a lot tougher than I expected. Soon enough I got used to everyone, though. I just had to come out of my shell and loosen up a bit.

I suppose fitting in with the Auckland rugby team was a bit of a challenge as well initially although I was helped because I knew a couple of the players through being in the New Zealand Secondary Schools team the previous two years. They did their best to make me feel welcome but a lot of the problems were of my own making. It came back to me being shy and finding it hard to talk to people. That was my fault, just the type of person I am and I couldn't help myself.

Two players made the world of difference – Junior Tonu'u and Martin Stanley, Joe's brother. Like me, they were also with Ponsonby as well as being in the Auckland squad. Marty would

Playing among so many greats for Auckland was a dream but it took time for me to settle in when I arrived in the big city.

always have a yarn with me, almost like a father figure. He was a bit older than me but not that much, only about six years or so. I started to call him Uncle Marty fairly quickly and I still do. I owe him a lot. He was awesome. At the first training run we had at Cornwall Park he was the first to come over to talk to me. You don't forget people who treat you well like that. And Junior made a point from the outset of keeping an eye on me as well.

Just how my move was all put together and who exactly did what, I couldn't say but I'd still linked up with one of New Zealand's most famous clubs in Ponsonby. I know club rugby is no longer the force it was in the days before the game went professional. That topic could be debated for hours and I'm not about to enter into it right now.

Ponsonby, though, stand for everything that's good about the strongest clubs. Talk about heritage – the word could have been invented with Ponsonby in mind. One of the more interesting ways of measuring All Black teams through the years, in any year, used to be to check off club representation. It's just about impossible to do that now. It's a rarity for top-level players to turn out for clubs. In fact, you might be stretched to link a club with lots of players. You just wouldn't know which isn't too desirable at all. But Ponsonby are right up there among the clubs with the most All Blacks.

Out of the players who appeared for Auckland at some stage in 1994, Ponsonby could claim Olo Brown, Martin and Jeremy Stanley, Brian Lima, Darren Kellett,

Jason Chandler, Junior Tonu'u, Shem Tatupu and Alf Uluinayau.

I certainly revelled in the club rugby scene with Ponsonby, and that must sound so strange now. A top-level player revelling in club rugby? It just doesn't fit, does it? Even playing it is a rarity let alone having the chance to revel in it.

While the rugby was more intense than what I'd become accustomed to, I actually found it easy in a strange way, mainly because the team was so well organised. Everyone did their own job which made it a lot more comfortable. There was no need to cover for anyone else, that's for sure. The rugby was more structured than what I'd been used to at home with evidence of a game plan being put into effective use. It was a big leap and that was just club rugby.

Ponsonby also had a fantastic team. The standard was brilliant although training conditions weren't necessarily that brilliant. We had just a couple of lights to train under. You could hardly see what you were doing then. When we were at the club, you'd see some of the famous faces, especially someone like B G Williams. Another bloke who was around was none other than Fats (Peter Fatialofa).

But the man on the Auckland rugby scene who would have the greatest influence on me was Auckland coach Graham Henry. It was really through him that I headed to Auckland. He got me started by encouraging me to come north.

Before I could worry too much about settling into Ponsonby and Auckland rugby, I was leaving the city for a new assignment in the game, and my biggest yet. My bloodlines had come into play – Wiki Spencer's little boy from Levin was packing his bags for an expedition to South Africa with the New Zealand Maori team. Again this was a case of a boy among men, me 18 and most of the other players in the squad aged from 25 up to 31. Among them were All Blacks Zinzan Brooke, the team's captain Arran Pene and Stu Forster but we were without a few more in Jamie Joseph, John Timu, Robin Brooke, Eric Rush, Dallas Seymour and Mark Cooksley. One of the other players selected was my Horowhenua teammate Graham Hurunui so there was one familiar face.

The mission was a tournament called the M-Net Nite Series in March involving South African provincial teams, the South African Development team, Namibia, Western Samoa and us. But for me it was more than a rugby trip, it was an experience going to a country like South Africa and one I made the most of, too. I loved the chance to tour there and, better still, I was able to take in the cultural significance of being in a Maori team.

On the rugby side, things didn't work out so well in the tournament when we could only draw our first game and were beaten by Eastern Province in the second, knocking us out of the event. There were a couple of other games, one against Griqualand West, the only match I appeared in and then at centre. We lost that one as well. I liked the rugby the Maori tried to play, though. They enjoyed throwing the ball around and all through my football days that's all I've really

In a team of so many stars, Zinny (Zinzan Brooke) was one of the biggest and also the captain of the great Auckland side of the mid-1990s.

Fitzy (Sean Fitzpatrick), being grabbed here by Rushie (Eric Rush), wasn't Auckland's captain but he still had a really big say in everything.

wanted to do.

The visit was all done and dusted in a couple of weeks and, before I knew it, I was back in Auckland playing for Ponsonby, gaining a taste of what to expect at a higher level. All the same, the step up to being involved with the Auckland team was huge. I knew it would be but the intensity surrounding the Auckland team was amazing.

At that stage, the Auckland guys were way out on their own as a unit. So they'd lost the Ranfurly Shield to Waikato late in the 1993 season... well that made little difference to Auckland being the ones who set the trends in New Zealand rugby.

We went on to win the NPC in 1994, 1995, 1996 and again in 1999 then, when the Super 12 started, the Blues won in 1996 and 1997 before losing the 1998 final. So for that period of five years – my first five years in Auckland – the achievement level was right up there.

The Ranfurly Shield was also reclaimed in 1995 and the atmosphere and everything connected with Auckland was incredible in those first few years. It didn't take me long to realise it was the perfect move, even though I had to endure a bit of pain before I felt remotely at home.

Walking into a dressing room and seeing all those players in the Auckland team, the ones I used to watch on TV, was fairly overwhelming at first. There were plenty of guys to be wary of in terms of seniority, like Fitzy (Sean Fitzpatrick), Zinny, Robin Brooke, Olo, Howie (Shane Howarth), Michael Jones, Lee Stensness, Richard Fromont, Eroni Clarke and Mark Carter. And, of course, JK (John Kirwan) was still there, too, that year before finishing up and switching to rugby league with the Warriors in 1995. There was a lot of leadership experience as well among that crew, with Fitzy then the All Black captain but Zinny leading Auckland. I had to pinch myself to check it really was me in there with them.

I suppose there might be a perception that Auckland's preparation for rep games would be way more professional than what we did in Horowhenua. Of course, there were differences, mainly because Auckland had far more resources. At the same time, we always did things well with the Horowhenua team in terms of basic preparation methods. Scotty Houston had us in camp the night before home games, just like we would with Auckland – but instead of staying in a four-star hotel, we'd be on a marae. I can tell you the food was much better on the marae!

The end result was still the same, though. In each setting we were together as a team focusing on what we had to do and preparing as well as we could. I liked being on the marae. I guess the fact we had quite a few Maori players in the side had something to do with going there but I found it quite relaxing – and it was probably free, too, which would have suited the Horowhenua Rugby Union. While the level of competition and the quality of players across the board was understandably markedly different I found the preparation aspects for a third division team were still comparable.

Where I would notice the world of difference was after the match. At home, there was a bit of a function put on with a few beers and something to eat. We'd be dressed up as such but wearing whatever tie you wanted and you'd just be down at the bar, have a feed of some spuds and peas and have a yarn. It was always fairly laid-back.

In Auckland, it was more formal and really ritzy, sponsors putting on functions where nothing was too much. We'd have to be there at a certain time, on show to people and dressed smart. In actual fact, that didn't put me out as much as people might have expected. That's because I'd been able to develop as a rugby player – and a person – by being picked to play for the New Zealand Colts and the New Zealand Secondary Schools. I was used to getting dressed in a more formal way through experiences we had at after-match functions with those teams so I didn't feel like a country boy who was a bit lost once I saw what went on at Auckland after-match functions.

Training regimes weren't too different apart from the fact in Auckland it was far more intensive, and it needed to be because the game was so totally changed from what I'd been used to. The competition at the level Auckland were playing at was a lot harder, so you had to be a lot fitter and a lot stronger. In the Horowhenua days, the guys wouldn't have touched weights. It was a case of just turning up to train or to play really. In Auckland there was all sorts going on. There was individual running you had to do during the week, weights and a whole lot of specific things you had to work on. You'd probably be at the gym a couple of times week.

When I first arrived we still trained only twice a week – usually a Tuesday and Thursday – so you always had extra stuff to do during the week and you'd do it because it was expected. If you'd been asked to do it back in Horowhenua you'd probably say: "Ah, no. Why bother? I'm not doing that." Playing was training. You could get away with not doing it down there.

My initial foray in the renowned blue and white hoops wasn't anything too special, certainly not the second of my first outings when we were beaten 15-13 by Western Samoa in what was then called the Super 10, the forerunner to the Super 12. We didn't do at all well in the Super 10, beating Waikato first but then losing our other three matches.

The game was so much quicker than anything I'd come across before, way quicker, but at the same time there was in a sense more time to do what you needed to because of the structure. You'd know well in advance what you were going to do next.

In coming into the Auckland side, I obviously realised I was a much different proposition at first five than Grant Fox had been all those years before. I had to fight to break into the team. University's Mark George had the first game of the season before I was given a crack, Lee Stensness had a few games there and even Shane Howarth was used at first five once. I guess Ted had to go through a bit of a sorting out process as he looked for a long-term replacement.

I was used 10 times that year and through most of the Air New Zealand NPC. I think I consciously played a little tighter than I had for Horowhenua, especially for the first two seasons when I was fairly careful. I didn't feel I should try to do too much until I was a couple of years into it. I'm sure I was a lot more restrained than I would be normally, mindful that I didn't want to come in trying to throw miracle balls from the outset. As the new kid on the block, I just had to take my time, work into it gradually and do the simple things well. That's what I was concentrating on. I didn't want to blow it there and then so for my part it was very much: "Yes sir, no sir, three bags full sir."

It wasn't anything to do with a lack of confidence it was more to do with trying to establish myself. It's what happens in any new environment. You tend to be a bit stand-offish, not sure what to do and so you worry about the basics first.

As an All Black or playing for Auckland, Foxy (Grant Fox) had few rivals – if any – but my style of play was obviously a lot different.

I was also a bit lucky in terms of the pranks department. None of the guys tried to get one over me, not something that I've remembered anyway. All I know is that I was dealt to in court sessions and everyone expects that. I would have been required to down a few beers then. There's no escaping that when rugby teams are in business. You never get off that kind of thing lightly.

Once I was comfortable with myself, the surroundings, the coach and the players, then I started getting a bit cheeky and bringing more of my game into it with

My collection of national team jerseys was building up after being selected for the New Zealand Secondary Schools, New Zealand Maori and the Colts.

the flair I had. It took time to come around to it but I made it eventually.

I think Ted also had to get used to me as well. After all, he'd had a very senior player to look to in Foxy. He'd been in the Auckland team since 1982 and had been an absolute fixture for all those years. The players were well used to his style as well and then a new boy comes along. It can be difficult and I suppose it was at times. I guess Ted needed to look at how I played, how he wanted me to play or what players he could bring in to fit around me. There was a lot to sort through at first.

Along the way, there were interludes appearing for three different national teams – with New Zealand Maori again and also the New Zealand Colts for the second year as well as the New Zealand Under-19s. It certainly made for a varied existence with plenty of changes in coaches and team-mates.

Mattie Blackburn was the Maori coach again for a two-match internal tour in early June including a match against Fiji. A lot of the players who'd been in the team for the South African trip were still in the side but there were plenty of changes as well with the likes of Timu, Glen Osborne, Rushie, Paul Cooke, Shane Howarth, Jamie Joseph, Mark Cooksley, Kevin Nepia and Norm Hewitt coming into the team. I played only in the lead-up game against Mid Canterbury, scoring two tries in a 58-13 win.

The next commitments removed me from consideration for Auckland's matches against Northland and Canterbury, the last being Auckland's first game in the Air New Zealand NPC.

Instead I had a solid month of rugby with players basically in my age range. First up it was the New Zealand Under-19s coached by Frank Oliver and then the New Zealand Colts under Lin Colling. I found it a little bit strange because one moment three of us were with the under-19s and the next we doubled up with the under-21s. Daryl Gibson was in both sides and so was Anton Oliver, who captained the under-19 side.

We had Cully with us in that under-19 team, too. It's interesting when you look back on it now – and remember what happened in 1999 with the All Blacks – that Cully played centre for that team and also did the goalkicking. Apart from those guys, we had Brad Fleming, James Kerr, Isitolo Maka, Andrew Blowers,

Royce Willis and Greg Feek. We wound up that three-match tour by belting our Australian equivalents 55-6.

The campaign with the colts was a step up from the previous year. Instead of observing, I was right in the firing line this time, and it also brought me head-to-head with someone who would often be blocking my way in future years – Andrew Mehrtens. I've never had a rivalry with Mehrts. That's how others have seen it but that's not how I look at it. We both happened to play the same position in the same era and the selectors of various teams made their choice. On that tour, it was my chance when I was picked for the so-called test against the Australians although Mehrts was far more experienced than me. After being the new kid in 1993 I also appreciated the heavier involvement on a tour comprising one game in Port Macquarie and the other two in Sydney.

I like looking back over teams like these a few years later because it reminds you of the successes we have with New Zealand rugby's system. Of the 10 backs in the squad, Cashy (Adrian Cashmore), Jonah (Lomu), Tana (Umaga), Daryl, Mehrts, Justin (Marshall), Todd Miller and me all ended up playing for New Zealand and Brendan Laney became a Scotland international.

All Blacks in the making from the pack were our captain Taine Randell, Chresten Davis, Kees Meeuws and Anton. Once again the results were decisively in our favour as well, winning all three including a 41-31 margin against the Australian Under-21s. It's only when you're lucky enough to be selected and play in teams of this type that you gain an understanding of how effective the New Zealand system is in this crucial development area. Ample investment is made in youth rugby and it should be. It makes a difference, too, when one team in a given year like this could later claim as many as 12 All Blacks.

Through playing for so many different teams and under different coaches, my rugby education certainly benefited. I also found myself teaming up with a variety of halfbacks which had to be helpful in terms of development and flexibility. In the space of a couple of months or so I played outside Shane Stone with the Maori, Scott Hansen and Blair Feeney with the New Zealand Under-19 side, Justin Marshall with the colts and Junior with Auckland. Earlier in the season, Jason Hewett was another halfback partner with Auckland.

Once the tours were out of the way, all energy switched to Auckland's cause in the NPC – and we had a hot year, too. Having won the title in 1993 but lost the shield, there was an absolute hunger to do it all again. To succeed, we'd have to do so without not just Foxy but some other really experienced players as well. Inga (Va'aiga Tuigamala) had switched to rugby league with Wigan and Steve McDowell had moved to Wellington. Also gone were former All Blacks Terry Wright and Bernie McCahill, who had played very little in 1993 in any case.

It turned out to be a top year and, as new boys, Cashy and I were more than happy to be part of it. The best part was that I was able to settle into a run of matches playing with Junior, five straight against Taranaki, King Country, North Harbour, Wellington and Otago. We finished comfortably ahead of Taranaki 34-15 and coasted to beat King Country 71-7, lost a fairly extraordinary clash with North Harbour 31-35 – Harbour's first win against Auckland – and then returned to big-scoring mood in accounting for Wellington 52-30 and Otago 46-30.

After missing the Counties match I was back for the last three as Waikato were beaten and so, too, were Otago in the semi-finals. With North Harbour progressing on the other side that created a final that the whole of Auckland had to be excited about – us against Harbour.

For a guy in his first season in Auckland I'd seen just what the rivalry meant in the round-robin match when Harbour beat us but that was just a tea party beside what happened in the NPC final at Onewa Doman. Battle of the Bridge? That wasn't the half of it. It wasn't at all pretty, a really bitter game in fact with fights all over the place which caused a hell of a lot of fuss in the days afterwards. But history records it as another title to Auckland as we won the match 22-16. In successive years I'd gone from winning the third division with Horowhenua to doing the same with Auckland in the first division and, whatever went on in the final, that couldn't be a bad thing.

I'd been exposed to a lot of rugby at various levels in my first year away from home and certainly felt I was heading the right way. I'd always thought it would be nice to play for the All Blacks from a long way back, not in the way of having this dream, just that I'd like to achieve it. No doubt I used to joke to my mates: "I'm going to be an All Black one day, bro." Whether I actually believed it at the time would have been another matter. It wasn't something I gave a lot of thought to.

But after being in Auckland just the one season I could tell I was in the best place to develop and to have the best chance of being noticed if I was to go further. I was feeling better about living there, too, after finding it so hard at the start of the year without my friends and family. Boy, I longed for home more than once. Luckily Mum and Dad made a few trips up and that helped me. They came to see a couple of the games I played and also encouraged me to grit it out. I was never at a point where I thought of going home. I wasn't going to let that happen.

But once I'd been in the city for a while, the best thing about it was that there was so much to do, no end of things to do. I loved that about it and I could never get around to doing it all either. At home, it was a case of wondering what you'd do next.

Having lived inland in Levin I also loved being near the water and there were plenty of places where that was possible in Auckland. I enjoyed that about the city. Given time to settle in, there was also a group of guys I gravitated towards – Cashy, Charlie Riechelmann, Junior and obviously Marty (Stanley) as well in the early days.

There might have been moments during a season like my first one in Auckland when other players would have sought some guidance or pointers about aspects of their game. A mentor, I guess. Someone you could sit down with and chat about all sorts of things. While that might have suited others, it wasn't for me. I never felt compelled to seek help from anyone even though I was in such a new environment. I've never really gone for that at all, always happy to do my own thing in that area. Maybe I've been a bit stubborn about it but I have tended to try to work through problem areas myself if anything has been bothering me. Instead of looking for guidance, I just try to work things out the way I see them and do it my way.

It's not that I was trying to be smart or anything like that. I was simply following the processes I'd been going through all my footballing life. That's how I had always been in Levin. I never asked for help. I think it was more a reflection of my personality and that shyness coming out along with a bit of that stubbornness I mentioned. My

Adrian Cashmore (Cashy) was a bit like me, coming to Auckland from the provinces.

style is to listen and digest, think about things and then do what needs to be done. I'm not a great one for talking things through in detail and over-analysing technical aspects.

If I had some sort of technical problem – maybe it was my goalkicking or it was a lack of distance on my kicks or something else – I would work on it myself trying to iron out whatever was wrong. I've been able to figure out the best way of improving my skills in all sorts of ways. I'll always observe when players are coming up with something new, say like the league players and the banana kick in more recent times. I'd see someone doing it and then go out and work out for myself how I could copy it and bring it into my game.

The kicking game is so much more refined now. In the past distance was just

Following pages: One thing about moving to Auckland from 1994 . . . it meant lots of success. And getting our hands back on the Ranfurly Shield in 1995 – that's me down in front with a hand literally on it – was huge.

about everything. A first five was looking to carve off as much territory as he could. Up-and-unders were absolute sky scrapers. Now the range of kicks used is so varied. What you might call touch kicks are used far more often, the well-placed little grubber kick through an advancing defensive line or the little chip over the top and you try to perfect pinpoint placement with bombs to give the chasers every show. A lot of that has come about through the changes in the laws of course. With the defences the way they are now, you have to look for other options.

Because of that, my kicking game is probably the one aspect I spend the most time on trying to improve. Passing takes care of itself because you're automatically working on that all the time in drills whereas kicking needs extra attention outside the regular training environment. Even if I'm playing around before, during or after training I'm testing myself by trying to bend the ball around a post or target, or trying to hit a target with kicks. You can never do enough of it and I keep working at it. I'll do that even when we're moving from one drill to another. I'll pick up a ball and try to put it on a spot I've identified.

Through my own means, observing others and playing for Ponsonby, Auckland, New Zealand Maori, New Zealand Colts and New Zealand Under-19s I was blotting up all sorts of information in 1994. It was a steep learning year but exactly what I expected being exposed to top coaching and also finding myself alongside some of the best players the game had ever seen. I was just two days past my 19th birthday when we won the NPC final, which said it all about how far I'd come so soon and I was really only just starting out.

Everyone says it: You have to put the work in practising your skills. And I do. I'm always working on areas of my game.

CHAPTER 5

A Man Named Ted

MOST COACHES leave some sort of an impression but I don't have a vivid recall of my experiences with every coach I had, mainly because I never spent too much time with some of them. Take Laurie Mains. I can't tell you a lot about his qualities as a coach because I was exposed to his methods only fleetingly when I first came into the All Blacks in 1995. I was barely 20 when I was called into the touring team as a replacement. I was basically only a midweek player then although I was a reserve for the test in Paris.

The same has happened throughout my career being involved with so many different coaches in a range of teams. In the New Zealand Colts, for instance, the coach changed in each of the three years I was in the team – Peter Thorburn first in 1993, Lin Colling in 1994 and in 1995 it was Ross Cooper. I was eligible for the colts again in 1996 but knee cartilage surgery ruled me out of contention; if I had been available, I would have had a new coach again. That's how the system works but, because I've never been a great one for remembering detail, the influence a lot of coaches have had on me is difficult to reflect. I simply can't tell you.

It's the same with a lot of specifics in most games I've played. There are players who can tell you just about everything that happened in game after game, the scores and all that kind of thing. Half the time, I struggle to recall the score of a game I played even last week let alone 10 years ago. Once they're over, most of them fade away, which is in keeping with my attitude of never dwelling on things, of wanting to look forward. As I'm always saying, I move on while everyone's still going over and over something you can't change.

But the mention of the colts and the year 1995 brings back some vivid recollections. Of course, the year itself registers because of the Rugby World Cup above all else. With the tournament happening early in the season in South Africa – starting in May – there was a big build-up for the All Blacks including a New Zealand trial and the return of the North Island–South Island match played in Dunedin.

I hadn't for a moment imagined I was an All Black contender at that stage but I was given a pointer that I was in the frame in some way after being selected to play for the North Island. In all, there were nine Auckland players in a side coached by Ted (Graham Henry) and, although I failed to last the game, I did score two tries in our 55–22 win. More importantly for me, I appreciated I'd been given an indication I was in the selectors' thinking or at least in their notebooks.

What became a highlight for me that year, though, was my third year in the New Zealand Colts, one which took me to Argentina to play in the Southern Hemisphere Under-21 tournament in July. One year it had been South Africa with the Maori, the next it was Argentina with the colts.

By now, of course, a pattern was emerging playing in sides like the colts. There was a core group of players I'd come up through the system with and this side wasn't short on supplying All Blacks of the future. Taine Randell was the captain for the second year running, he and I being the only players who'd been in the colts for three consecutive years. The other All Blacks in the making were Daryl Gibson, Chresten Davis, Kees Meeuws and Anton Oliver – all backing up from 1994 – plus Christian Cullen, Roger Randle, Jeremy Stanley, Danny Lee, Mark Robinson (the halfback), Andrew Blowers, Isitolo Maka, Scott Roberston, Dion Waller and Carl Hoeft. That had to make it a hell of a good team with so many players going on with it.

And with that talent, the rugby side of the tour was great as we beat Argentina first and then South Africa to make the final against Australia, where we came out 33–16 ahead with Cully scoring two of our five tries.

But for all the success we had, the strongest memories of the trip are of the country itself. It's not one of the most appealing places you'll see, well certainly Buenos Aires isn't and that's where we were located throughout the tournament. It was a long way to the venue from where we were staying in the centre of the city, about an hour and a half out as I recall it. And there was just so much poverty almost everywhere we went. The city was really scruffy and scungy. It didn't stop the boys having a good time. We had heaps of fun besides enjoying the rugby. And we were certainly treated – and fed – well. We'd heard stories from the past and we soon found out for ourselves, that they sure do feed you in Argentina. Some of the barbies we had were unreal, the steaks were awesome.

Ted (Graham Henry) with quite a bit of hair. That shows you how long he's been around now but he's the coach I've learnt the most from.

This was one time when I did remember the coaching as well, which is a bit unusual because there's not generally a lot you can learn from a coach when you're working with them for such a short period of time. In a way they become just another coach. But with the colts in 1995 it was different. We had a full-on programme rather than just two of three matches on an internal tour or to Australia. It started with the South Pacific Under-21 quadrangular tournament before we headed to Argentina so it meant there was a lot more time to see how Ross Cooper operated as the head coach. Fairly soon he would be involved with the All Blacks and I must say I thought he was a decent coach. He brought a lot to the side and he was also a nice guy – down to earth, a bloke from the country like me.

What really develops on tours of that type, and through being selected in teams with the same guys more than once, are the real friendships. Cully was one of them, of course. Coming from the same part of the country we always had a bit in common but there were plenty of others I got to know really well, too, because we were seeing a fair bit of each other.

But there's one person I reckon I've seen more of than any other in my time playing rugby. That's obviously Graham Henry. From 1994 through to 1998 he was my coach with Auckland or the Blues – and mostly both – before returning to work in a new role with Auckland and the Blues again a couple of years ago. I wouldn't want to think about how many matches and training runs I've had with him. Someone else can count them.

It didn't take long for me to realise Ted would become the most important coach of my career. Given I have played so much rugby under his direction, that probably stands to reason but he's proved time and again to me and everyone who's been involved with him that he's a coach who has so many all-round strengths. The fact he has sustained such a high level of performance over such a long period of time also says a lot for his quality as a coach.

The first time I came into direct contact with Ted in 1994 he was well set as Auckland coach after taking over from Maurice Trapp in 1992. From that moment, it struck me how organised he was.

I'm not saying other coaches weren't but Ted was at another level in that area from anything I'd previously seen, and I haven't seen anyone to match him since either.

It would start before every training run, when he always brought the players in for an early session on the whiteboard, laying out what training would consist of and he'd always have something noted down about the opposition and what they would try to do.

The first key point I noticed was that he always knew what the opposition would throw at us. He must have spent endless hours looking at videos in those

During the Auckland and Blues reign in the mid-1990s, Ted was in command. He could handle all aspects of the coaching game.

days because the computer technology wouldn't have been what it is today when everything can be brought up on a laptop. His only option was to do all his analysis by TV and video.

At the whiteboard session he'd run through the opposition's moves and explain it all in detail then out on the training field, he would run a version of the opposition against the playing side and have that line-up running the opposition's moves at us. He strove to ensure everyone was clear on what we were doing and hopefully what the opposition would be doing.

He was completely different from anything I'd come across before, the first coach I encountered who was really into detailed analysis in every sense. In his whiteboard sessions he really talked things through with us but he was the first coach I'd seen who could mix it up between whiteboard work and video analysis yet still be able to show what was required out on the training field.

You hear all the time how some coaches say they don't take any notice of the opposition and that their only concentration is on their own team. Sometimes that may need to be the case when a coach knows his team is performing badly and he can't afford to do anything but worry about trying to fix up whatever's wrong. But today coaches can't afford to look only at their team and ignore or pay limited attention to the opposition.

You need to know what teams do in certain situations, what part of the field they do it in and you need to be aware of their set moves. Ted has always made

Ball in hand, running free – that's always the way I've liked it. It was a big change for me to come into the Auckland team but in time I revelled in it.

it his business to do that, if not a priority. And I'd say the results of the work he does in that area show he gets it right far more often than not. We won the NPC title a few times back in my early years in Auckland so something must have been working.

It had to be said we had some damned good players as well. They were onto it and knew their jobs as well as anyone around. It's one thing to have a game plan and another to have the players who are capable of seeing it through but to me Ted always found the balance of the right game plan for the players he had. That was the secret. Certainly Auckland rugby had been in good shape for quite a few years before that as well so they were great times to be involved. It wasn't too hard a job for Ted to fit into, especially with all the experienced players he had there when he first started.

But going into 1994 he was without a player who'd been so vital to everything Auckland had done for so long – Grant Fox. I suppose that put some sort of heat on me being the replacement. I'd say I was more nervous about it than anything. It wasn't a case of thinking who I was following. That's not the way I am. It was more about the challenge I had in front of me, being young still and coming into a team like Auckland. It was a fairly big change for a boy from Horowhenua. I just wanted to do everything by the players I had around me then. I didn't want

Of all the halfbacks I've played with Junior (Tonu'u) was just awesome, firing out massive passes that make a first five's life so much easier.

to let them down.

As the coach, Graham was obviously critical to the way I fitted into the side after Foxy finished. The players helped in that regard as well, including the senior pros like Fitzy. They all wished me all the best and wanted me to enjoy myself in the team.

I suppose as far as first fives go, there was quite a change from what Foxy brought to the team and what I did. Auckland's style had been built around the way Foxy played for years but I arrived as more of a running first five, which made it a bit of a challenge initially I guess.

In the first few years in Auckland I had to work with various halfbacks including Jason Hewett, Junior Tonu'u, Brett Iti and Tu Nu'uali'itia. They all brought strengths to their game but Junior was awesome to work in with. The great thing about him was that he'd just fire the ball out to you with that huge pass of his.

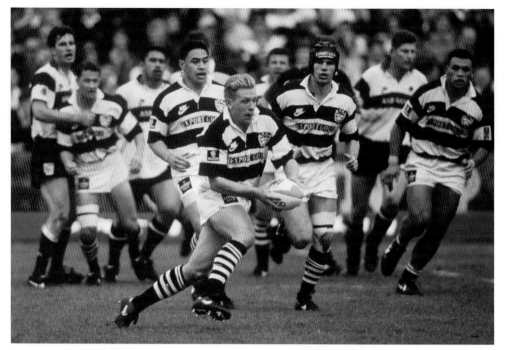

Starting out with Auckland, it was great to have experienced and steadying influences around me, especially Stainless (Lee Stensness) at second five.

There hasn't been a better passer of the ball in my time and I don't think there ever will be either.

It was a fantastic way for me to start having someone like Junior there, even though I'd never had anything to do with him before. With the pack going forward all the time and then bullet passes from JT, you couldn't ask for much more than that when you're a first five. It was just bloody awesome.

Through that early period our midfield backs included Lee Stensness, Martin Stanley, Eroni Clarke and Johnny Ngauamo. With Stainless (Stensness) there outside me and JT at halfback I had two experienced players to rely on. We had Eroni out there as well, although often on the wing, and Cashy (Adrian Cashmore) or Howie (Shane Howarth) at fullback. There was a really good balance out on the field for someone like me still new to the scene.

But Ted was the ringmaster. With his background as a principal there were lots of signs of the school teacher at work in the way he arranged and organised everything but he never did in a schoolmasterly way. Nothing like it, not from my viewpoint anyway. I suppose there is a danger that coaches who have been teachers can be seen to be too over the top with discipline but there was never an issue with that with Henry.

My memory of him on a one-on-one basis in those days is that he didn't sit me down to tell me what I should and shouldn't be doing. At the level I'm at now I tend to be left to do things my own way. It would have been different then when I was so young but I don't recall being given specific directions. While I'd come to Auckland immediately after Foxy had finished his career, there was nothing done directly with him either.

It had to be said everything went superbly for my first three seasons playing for Ted in Auckland. After winning the NPC all but unchallenged in 1994, it was more of the same in 1995 although we weren't flash early on when we beat Wellington narrowly and then lost again to North Harbour (11-12). From there on, we put together a winning sequence although not without some frights against Otago (25-21) and Southland (21-19) before pasting Canterbury 35-0 to regain the Ranfurly Shield. That was sweet. We defended it against Waikato, avenged our loss to Harbour with a 60-26 in the NPC semi-finals to book another final. Once more, it was a controversial one, too. Not for fighting this time but for the penalty try Colin Hawke awarded as we won 23-19. It certainly gave everyone something to talk about.

For Ted and us, 1996 was better again because there was now a new prize to fight for as the world of professional rugby kicked in. More recently the season had started with the Super 10 which didn't really create too much excitement but having the Super 12 as a structured competition involving franchises from New Zealand, Australia and South Africa was the biggest thing we'd had. And, of course, we were being paid. Things had certainly moved on quickly from when I started; that form teacher from my days at Waiopehu College must have been regretting what he'd said to me a few years earlier. There I was at 20, in only my third year out of school, being paid to play rugby. It was all a bit unbelievable at first.

Of course, it changed the entire playing field. Attitudes to training had to change as well from the coaching staff right down to the players. The old routine of essentially training twice a week – and doing that late in the afternoon or evening – became a thing of the past as we tried to adapt to what other professional sports have been doing for years. Ted was switched onto the requirements from the outset and, in many ways, we – then officially called the Auckland Blues – had a bit of a jump on the field in the Super 12. That's certainly the way it looked as the first year unfolded. I'm not saying we were way ahead of our opponents but by the end of the short Super 12 competition it was clear we'd done things fairly well, certainly a lot better than the other New Zealand franchises. The Waikato Chiefs were the next best in sixth place, the Otago Highlanders were eighth, the Wellington Hurricanes ninth and the Canterbury Crusaders were dead last, which you'd never credit the way they developed. In many ways that emphasises the point, though. When the Super 12 started, the Blues were ready for it but the other New Zealand teams took a little time to get up and running.

We loved the chance to show our stuff in a competition that was so heavily

When the Super 12 came along, we started life as the Auckland Blues. These days we're just the Blues – and haven't the jerseys changed a lot?

weighted towards attacking rugby. The defence was a bit loose but that didn't bother us because we had such a strong attack to rely on.

With Mac McCallion as his assistant, Henry was at his best for this. They had decent playing material with a pack of All Black quality – Zinny, Andrew Blowers and Michael Jones were the usual loose forward combination, Robin Brooke and Charlie Riechelmann the locks and then there was the front row any side would kill for of Craig Dowd, Sean Fitzpatrick and Olo Brown. Head out through the backline and Junior sparked it all while our midfield was Stainless and Eroni, Cashy was at full back and our real weapons were on the wings – the two big guys Jonah (Lomu) and Joeli (Vidiri).

We didn't run through every opponent we encountered. There were, for instance, a few setbacks on the road losing 34-40 to Brumbies (or the ACT Brumbies as they were officially then) in Canberra, an ugly 13-51 loss to the Queensland Reds in Brisbane – we still haven't beaten them there – and a 22-34 reverse against Transvaal in Johannesburg. But there were some huge scores in other matches when we scored 30 or more points in every match we won, ultimately accounting for Northern Transvaal 48-11 in the semi-finals and then Natal 45-21 to claim the trophy. Sweet.

Bathing in the glow of success . . . Charlie (Riechelmann) and I with the trophy after the Blues beat the Brumbies in the 1997 Super 12 final.

With Auckland, Ted lost the Ranfurly Shield to Taranaki, reclaimed it from Waikato later in the season and then guided the team to another NPC title win with a 46-15 victory over Counties-Manukau in the final. I was beginning to like the pattern here. There was plenty to like with the wins flowing like this.

On the face of it, 1997 was looking like more of the same and, while the rest of the country mightn't have liked the Blues and Auckland dominating rugby this way, those of us inside the two teams were more than keen to keep it going. That's the way it started, too, when the Blues warmed up for the second edition of the Super 12 with a Northern Hemisphere tour in February by beating a Bristol XV, Harlequins and Brive.

That was the springboard for an all but perfect Super 12 campaign. Remembering we were without Jonah after he'd been diagnosed with his kidney condition, this proved to be an exceptional effort. Our attack was still really potent – again we topped 500 points – but we tightened up our defence and emerged with a second successive crown by beating the Brumbies 23-7 in the final. Just one match prevented us having a clean slate of 13 straight wins, coming in the opening round with an amazing 40-40 draw with the Northern Transvaal Blue Bulls in Pretoria.

But outstanding as the Blues were in the Super 12, when we put our Auckland jerseys on later in the year we weren't quite up to the mark in the Air New Zealand NPC. For one, we lost the Ranfurly Shield again, beaten 31-29 by Waikato in a decent battle with the wrong result. And we faltered at the semi-final stage in the NPC when Canterbury eliminated us.

Whether that indicated the balance of power was starting to shift, I don't know.

I've always liked to try something different, like the kick off the knee. It doesn't matter whether I'm playing in a test match or a Super 12 game, everything's worth a try.

It shouldn't have, although it's a fair point that we suffered a couple of heavy blows on the player front as we aimed for a third straight win in the Super 12. Zinny moved on, going to Britain, and Fitzy had on-going problems with his knee injury and didn't play at all in our 1998 campaign. On the positive side, Jonah was restored after his illness problems.

While we started with a loss to the Coastal Sharks – who used to be Natal – and were also beaten again by the Reds at Ballymore, we still qualified top and moved into the final which, for the third year running, was at our place, Eden Park. It was also the first all-New Zealand final with the Crusaders winning through in the other semi.

It was also obvious that season that a lot of the other sides were starting to catch us up. When the Super 12 started in 1996, Graham had us ahead of everyone else in terms of what we were doing but I think other sides were beginning to adapt to our approach and were finding ways of closing the gap.

In that 1998 final, the Crusaders had a game plan that revolved strongly around defence, probably more so than any other side. We had set ourselves up as an attacking force when the Super 12 arrived. That was our plan and we scored heaps of points. That was the nature of the Super 12 in general for the first couple of seasons until it started to tighten up, probably more so through the Crusaders than any other side.

With Jonah and Joeli on the wings plus Cashy at fullback we had some real fire-power. You have to use players like them when they're there and we did. Of course, it all depends on the forward pack you have and we were lucky enough that we had a very good set of forwards in front of us. Take a look at the Hurricanes. They had a decent backline but used to struggle because they didn't really have the forwards to give them go-forward ball so they could get it out wide.

The Crusaders had our number in the 1998 final. We were still able to put a decent side out against them but they had a fantastic pack and they just kept coming at us all day. Look, let's not go there. There's that moment I can't forget when Junior (Tonu'u) and I were caught out by the bounce of the ball... and James Kerr got that try. Yeah, it was awful and the Crusaders went on to win 20-13.

What we didn't know was that a huge development was about to change the entire complexion of Auckland and Blues rugby. The man who had done so much to make a difference was about to leave us and take his talents to coach Wales.

It came as more than a bit of a bolt when Ted left halfway through the year for Cardiff. I don't recall him saying anything to us about feeling there was nowhere else to go in New Zealand rugby. Certainly that was the talk that his ambition to coach the All Blacks was unlikely to come about any time soon with John Hart in that job. Ted's departure was obviously a huge loss to Auckland rugby. Obviously he wanted to have a shot at coaching the All Blacks but the chance

**Wales and leeks are on the menu as Ted sizes up his new rugby challenge in the United Kingdom.
We wished him all the best.**

wasn't there for him. We all knew he wanted to coach internationally and when
he landed the position with Wales I just thought: "Good on him".

The upshot of his departure was understandably one of panic in Auckland
rugby. The NPC was only weeks away from beginning and the union had lost a
champion coach. Maurice Trapp had coached Auckland so successfully with
Bryan Williams immediately before Ted took over and he answered the call to
come back in a caretaker role. It was going to be a hell of job, especially with the
first NPC match also being a Ranfurly Shield challenge against Waikato and
Auckland's All Blacks all unavailable because they were on Tri Nations duty in
South Africa at the time.

The season turned into a disaster, Auckland winning only four games and losing five to finish eighth in the NPC, the worst result since the competition had
begun in 1976. The records showed it had been almost 50 years since Auckland
had finished with more losses than wins in a season. Ironically, the second-string
side was very close to a shock win in the shield challenge against Waikato, losing
just 23-24, but later there were some terrible losses to Canterbury (17-50),
Counties-Manukau (29-45) and North Harbour (12-32).

There could be no argument that Ted's sudden departure impacted on the side.

We'd been so in tune with his methods. We were always going to be up against it once this all happened but it didn't make it any easier to take after the outstanding successes we'd achieved season after season.

When Ted went to coach Wales I guess we were at the end of an era really. That would become more obvious over the next few years as efforts turned to trying to halt the sudden slide. From the top, we'd crashed and it would require a lot of rebuilding before the Blues and Auckland would fully recover.

We were still in the early stages of professional rugby at that time and there might have been some thinking that Graham Henry's decision to coach a rival nation like Wales didn't stack up too well. In actual fact, professional sport is about pursuing the best opportunities open to you. The old-fashioned attitude about loyalty can still come into play but really you have to take what is best for you and your future. It's your living. So it didn't bother me at all that Graham was heading to Wales.

While the player roster for Auckland and therefore the Blues was still fairly sound in 1998 we had been going through changes around that time with senior players gone or about to leave. That was inevitable. The way I saw it, it was just one of those phases teams go through from time to time when players move on, the coach goes and you start all over again.

Obviously I had a hell of a lot to thank Graham for in those early years with the Blues and Auckland and I certainly had a bit of an interest in seeing how Wales went once he began working with them. It was definitely pleasing to see the results he had, especially early on. That showed what sort of a coach he was and what he could do with a side like Wales. Let's be honest, the Welsh weren't too good back then. They were in poor shape and even though Ted didn't have much talent to work with he was still able to turn Welsh rugby around. It was a huge credit to him.

It was disappointing, though, that later he had to endure all the business with Grannygate over using Shane Howarth, but I can't say I really worried about that too much. I felt sorry for Graham and his family that they had to go through that because it wasn't a nice way to finish off with Wales. Then again, that's the way it is with professional rugby I suppose.

With his school teacher background, his sense of being so organised with both the Blues and Auckland shouldn't have been such a surprise. What we didn't see, which you can do with teachers, is someone who was over the top in the area of discipline. In truth discipline in the team then was led by the players, not by Graham. Both on the field and off it, the senior guys showed the way in that area and we didn't have any real issues with it during that period.

We actually had two principals around Auckland teams in those days with John Graham coaching the forwards. I know he certainly had a reputation as a disciplinarian but we never saw it that way when he worked with us.

What we also had in both of them was two coaches who were more mature, you could say. In fact, when Ted was named as All Black coach in December, 2003, there were people who began to question whether he might be too old for the position, pointing out he would be 61 by the time of the next World Cup in 2007 if he still has the job. That just doesn't add up at all. The age of a coach has nothing at all to do with it. I don't care at all how old a coach is. What it comes down to is whether he can do the job, whether he knows the game and can relate to the players.

What I look for in a coach is that he's well organised most of all and that his preparation for each team is on the mark. I think a coach needs to be fairly relaxed and he has to be able to let the guys enjoy themselves, to be capable of maintaining that relaxed atmosphere. Even though we're now in the professional era I haven't noticed a change in attitude among players or coaches in terms of having a passion and enthusiasm for the game. That's still there as strongly as it ever was.

Personally, I'm not too worried about whether a coach is able to analyse me and know what makes me work. I think I do a decent job of that myself. I know what's required to put me in the right frame for a game. A coach can help but a lot of the responsibility for preparing properly for a match must come back to each player.

To be honest I actually don't like talking to coaches. I like to stay out of their way – and I like them to stay out of my way as well. Nothing against them at all, it's just that I don't like getting close to coaches. I prefer to maintain a distance. I don't have a lot to say to them. If they say something to me and I want to listen to it, I'll digest it. If I don't want to listen it will go in one ear and out the other. That's the way I've always been.

What I'm trying to say is that I prefer coaches who have something meaningful to say, who don't just talk for the sake of it. There's nothing worse than that and there have been lots of coaches who are like that. I can't recall any issues I've had with any coaches over the way I might have played, something I may have done in a game that I shouldn't have. Basically coaches know what sort of player I am and what sort of person I am and they respect that.

It's always the case in any team that some players need to be treated differently by the coach. I know how I operate but I also appreciate there are players who need to be propped up by the coach or calmed down. Some are more on edge and need a bit more work or a bit more attention paid to them.

What I have discovered is that a lot of the younger players today are far more relaxed about the way they conduct themselves. They like to keep it nice and calm which is the way I prefer it. They enjoy themselves more and aren't so uptight, which isn't always the case with some of the older ones. At times some of them do take themselves a bit too seriously. With today's newer faces they have a lot of fun and when it's time to switch on they do. As ever it's always about having the right balance and they seem to have it.

The traditional way of building up to big games, especially test matches, was to keep everything wound up all week. That doesn't suit me. I like to have things running calmly for most of the week, even on the bus on the way to the ground and then, once you arrive at the venue, you can switch on.

I will think about a game at certain times during the week. In fact, individual preparation is the most important part of any build-up. In a team environment it's best to stay loose and enjoy yourselves during the week but when you're on your own you can become a little more intense about it all and go over what you need to do.

Much of the time I try to control the level of mental input into a match. It tends to be something I do at night-time, especially at home, maybe when I'm sitting in the spa. During the day I try to keep busy doing things so I don't need to sit around concentrating on it too much. I might shoot off on my motorbike and just let everything go or I could be at home doing some cleaning or other house work, walking the dogs. Anything I can find to do actually. That's what keeps me occupied and relaxed.

We all know we have to respect each other and the way we all want to build up for a game. If some guys want to be silly buggers and others want to be serious about how they prepare, then they can go somewhere else to act up. You can bet it's the forwards who want it all staunch and serious. The good old tight five. That's the way they have been all through the years and nothing much changes. It works for them, and that's fine – as long as they let me do what works for me.

That doesn't mean there aren't set times for when the team is all that matters. There are events we should all go to and times when we should all be together. That is as valuable as ever even in the professional era.

I always found those key areas functioned well under Ted's coaching operation. He had a full understanding of what was required. Now he's back as All Black coach and I couldn't be happier for him. He deserves the chance as much, if not more, than anyone.

It hopefully means his greatest contribution to New Zealand rugby is still to come, although it can be said he has already contributed an awful lot with the way he started the Blues off in the Super 12. He led the way in showing how the game could be played in those first few seasons. He has also brought through a lot of fantastic players both in his Auckland NPC teams and in the Blues. They're players who have gone on to be big things.

You only have to look at what happened to the All Blacks on the back of what the Blues did in the first three years of the Super 12. We had so many All Blacks

By 2004, Ted was back home and this time in the job he'd always wanted as All Black coach. He'd made Tana Umaga the new captain, too.

back then, around 10 or 11 in squads in 1997 for instance.

After Graham left for Wales, the loss of some senior players and the deterioration in the Blues' and Auckland's efforts impacted dramatically on All Black teams. It reached the point in 2001 where Dougy (Howlett) was the only Auckland player in the All Black squad for the Tri Nations Cup campaign and for the end of year tour to Ireland, Scotland and Argentina.

But look what happened when Ted returned from Wales and took on a role with the coaching team for Auckland and then the Blues. In almost no time at all, Auckland's All Black fortunes coincidentally sky-rocketed, so much so there were 10 Aucklanders in the 2003 Rugby World Cup squad. It wasn't through his deeds alone that Auckland and the Blues tasted success again in 2002 and 2003 but he still showed once more the special ability he has to make players and teams into something.

CHAPTER 6

Showing the Faith

A TEENAGED KID FROM HOROWHENUA wouldn't normally expect to need a lawyer, well not a guy like me who stayed out of trouble. I'd never been in a lawyer's office and wasn't in any hurry to find out what the experience was like.

But something came up in 1995 and the next thing I knew I was walking into this glass tower in downtown Auckland, taking a lift to the sky and wondering what part of the real world this was. Rugby's face was changing forever and that's the reason I was joining a few other players to try to understand what was going on and to figure out what we would do.

This was why Auckland commercial lawyer, David Jones, came into my life. Forget the formal name, though, because I've really known him only as "DOJ", pronounced like "Dodge". If you hadn't guessed, his nickname comes from his initials and he's been involved in my football career ever since, not as a player manager or agent as many of them are called, but as my lawyer or counsel. He advises me and helps me in all sorts of ways.

In 1995 he didn't need to help me alone but a bunch of my other Auckland team-mates as well. I was only 19 when I walked into DOJ's offices for the first time. To say we were all a bit overwhelmed would have been a bit of an understatement.

> **DOJ:** *"I remember the first time they came to see me their eyes seemed to be as big as saucers. There appeared to be a degree of apprehension as to what they were getting into — a fear of the unknown perhaps. This was an environment they'd never been in before."*

It certainly was an eye-opener but our minds were also full of all sorts of thoughts about what we had in front of us, not so much DOJ's offices but the fact our own rugby futures were unknown. Something was there for us. We just didn't know which way to go.

The All Blacks were at the World Cup in South Africa at the time and there was lots of talk about what could be on offer. It was mid-1995 when News Limited had come onto the scene, pumping millions of dollars into rugby union to take it into the professional age. They'd made their big announcement just as the Rugby World Cup final was about to be played at Ellis Park in Johannesburg in late June. It had been quite a year for the rugby codes because, only a few months earlier, News Limited had also made a move in rugby league spending millions on their Super League plan. So things were happening there in a huge way. There were lots of rugby league offers around for union players as well. It was hard to keep up with it all.

At the same time, the World Rugby Corporation had made their presence felt with their proposal to make the game far more global with the promise to pay players more money than a lot of us could begin to believe. This really started to gather pace during the All Blacks' two Bledisloe Cup tests against Australia in July. Earlier the WRC had been approaching players with contracts and suddenly the New Zealand Rugby Union was fighting to keep hold of players all over the country. That's why I was with the group of players in a lawyer's office.

DOJ: *"Junior Tonu'u came to see me with his contract and said: 'There are a whole a lot of other boys who don't know what to do either. Can I bring them along to talk to you?' Of course, I said.*
"So, I had a deputation that came to see me with these NZRU contracts as well as the WRC contracts. There was Junior, Eroni Clarke, Johnny Ngauamo, Waisake Sotutu, Adrian Cashmore, Carlos and one or two others. It was effectively the Auckland backline."

Andy Haden had given us all WRC contracts and there were plenty of questions we had about them. One of the issues for us was that the WRC contracts always mentioned only US dollars but they were obviously a lot bigger than what the NZRU contracts were worth.

So, with the group of guys, we had our first meeting with DOJ. He was great right from the start because he made everything clear for us and put our minds at ease really. He started by saying: "It's not just money. Let's have a look at the pros and cons."

Using a whiteboard, he listed each contract plus the key points of what each of them had to offer and then we went through a process of comparing them on a

DOJ (David Jones) has played an awesome part in my life, both in rugby and outside it. I can't say enough about him.

point by point basis. There were some things we still couldn't be at all certain about. In the WRC set-up there was the question of where we might end up playing. If you didn't make the New Zealand team or the reserves, then the organisation could place you in one of the other conferences, as they were called. It was all based a lot on the models used in American sports where they have conferences in the NFL, the NBA and so on. The point to be taken from this was that you could end up playing in a conference in the United States, somewhere in Europe or wherever. That was a negative because it created uncertainty.

DOJ: *"I made it graphic for them: 'If the WRC gets off the ground and you stay with the NZRU, then you guys are likely to become All Blacks. If you go to the WRC, where you currently sit as rugby players, you're going to have a question mark over where you're going to play'. The other uncertainty with the WRC was that you didn't know what was going to happen because they didn't have their* *money. The whole deal was conditional on the WRC raising a huge sum of finance by a certain date, so I told them: 'If you sign this contract, you'll actually be waiting to see whether you've got a deal. If you sign the NZRU contract, then you have a deal'.*

"That wasn't all we had to worry about. When the guys came to see me, a lot of them also had rugby league offers as well as the rugby ones. Junior may have had one from Wigan and Adrian had a Bulldogs offer and another one as well while I recall Johnny also having a league offer. That's because so much was going on with Super League and the Australian Rugby League trying to buy players.

"It wasn't easy for these guys. Between them they had not only offers from the WRC and the NZRU but also league offers. I started by staying: 'Rather than having all these contracts on the table at once, do we push the league offers to the back? You want to play rugby, don't you? So, if we can't make something work with your rugby contracts, then the league ones are your fallback options'."

DOJ was open-minded about the options. He was just trying to spell out the detail so we had all the information. While signing a contract with the NZRU meant we'd have something solid, the money wasn't nearly as good. He also told us that, at the end of the day, we would simply have to make our own judgment on what we wanted to do and where we thought we should go. He said the biggest thing we needed was certainty. We had quite a few meetings with DOJ without making any quick decision and he also encouraged us to consider having representatives from the NZRU and the WRC to talk to us about the pros and cons of their offers.

Junior, being five years older than me and with a lot more experience, had told DOJ something else – and I knew exactly what he meant, too. He said he was concerned about the All Black clique in the Auckland team. At the time we had so many senior guys who'd been around for so many years and they were obviously deeply involved in what was going on with the WRC. You noticed guys like Sean Fitzpatrick, Zinzan Brooke and others obviously had something going on to do with the rebel organisation. Junior told DOJ he didn't know where we stood because the senior All Black guys were having a lot of meetings among themselves over what was taking shape. We didn't feel left out as such, it's just that we were the younger guys I guess and they probably thought they knew the best way how to handle the business.

DOJ: *"I spoke to Geoff Levy a couple of times who put me on to Andy Haden, who was the WRC person on the ground with Eric Rush (Rushie) in New Zealand. I also got hold of Rob Fisher from the NZRU and said to him: 'I've got the Auckland backline here. You might want to come and talk to them'. 'Yep',* *he said. Rob was over that fast it was almost like our offices were connected by a flying fox."*

DOJ arranged a series of meetings with Rob and we also met with the Auckland Rugby Union's CEO Murray Wright, Auckland coach Graham Henry and the Auckland team's manager Rex Davy. They all wanted to be involved in talking things through with us. There were also telephone meetings with people like Richard Crawshaw at the NZRU.

One way or another, we were touching base with as many people as possible to ensure we had plenty of information at our disposal. By now we had a decent understanding of what it all meant but we needed to be absolutely sure we were going to do the right thing for ourselves. It was a really important time in our careers.

DOJ checked out some other details like insurance. Both contracts had grey areas and he wanted to find out more about some of the various points and what was provided in terms of additional benefits and basic needs.

He stressed it wasn't his job to make the decision for us although he was more than prepared to pass on his opinion if we asked him for it. I suppose he didn't want to be seen to be trying to sell one proposal over the other. He wanted to be sure we understood the good and bad points of both offers so we could make an informed decision.

I actually did ask him directly for his view in the end and he told me: "I think it's a bird in the hand for me... the fact of the matter is, if you stay and the WRC gets off the ground, then you know you'll be All Blacks, you know what your income's going to be and you know you're going to be in New Zealand. There's probably no real downside because, if the WRC goes ahead and the NZRU doesn't succeed, the WRC will probably pick you up anyway and at some stage they'll be looking for new players as well. What you're doing is you're being loyal to New Zealand and you're going to be there for the All Blacks so, if you put all those things in a row, you're probably better to stay from a commercial viewpoint."

There's no question the NZRU's future was in the balance during this time in 1995. Who knows what would have happened if the WRC had flown. But talking to Rob Fisher was valuable. We felt comfortable because he was an Auckland person, telling us he wanted us to stay.

DOJ: *"From there it became a matter of negotiation with the guys saying: 'If we stay then you can't treat us as C players'. Rob Fisher was there constantly. I said to him: 'We're not going to hold you to ransom, we know you have budgets but don't pretend these guys aren't category A players. They're the Auckland backline'.*

New Zealand rugby boss Rob Fisher played a big part in convincing me – and a lot of my Auckland team-mates – to stick with the New Zealand Rugby Union in 1995.

Just through sensible negotiations we got it to a level where everyone was happy. It was a very sensible commercial process. Rob was just great during the process.
"I didn't think Rob got the recognition he deserved for helping to save the day because it was him who persuaded the guys to commit to New Zealand and he finally signed them. Then everything started to fall into place for New Zealand rugby."

There had been strong signs the NZRU was in real trouble over this before DOJ arranged for us to meet Rob. There'd been plenty of talk around that they were really struggling to attract any players to sign with the NZRU with so many guys lining up with the WRC. We could tell Rob was really relieved when he had the chance to talk to us. By winning us over he was basically able to save New Zealand rugby and that wasn't an exaggeration at the time.

The NZRU needed Auckland players to fall in with them. They couldn't succeed without them. The current All Blacks were certainly aligned to the WRC. They seemed to be solidly in behind the rebel organisation but we became the trigger for the change of heart. That's the way I saw it. After we decided to stick with the NZRU, Jeff Wilson and Josh Kronfeld switched very soon afterwards and then it all started happening. They didn't make some of the other All Blacks too happy with their decision at the time but that's the way it goes. I thought they'd all made a deal to stick together, only it changed at a late stage.

I didn't feel like I was in the middle of something really big. I wasn't too nervous or fazed about it. At the time, I could easily have gone either way because I didn't know any better and I was relatively young. But once we all got together with DOJ and talked things through I saw the picture a bit differently.

I don't know whether the WRC would ever have gone ahead anyway, even if I had signed. It didn't seem to have enough backing to get it started. It was real pie in the sky, a great concept possibly but trying to make it work would have been something entirely different.

The most important aspects to emerge from the experience were that we now had some order in our rugby lives and it was incredibly valuable – but a heck of a learning curve for a 19-year-old – to go through it all. Even better was the link it established for me, and for all the guys, with DOJ.

> **DOJ:** *"The very first time I saw Carlos he was like a number of them. He was overawed and he didn't say much. But I could see he was taking it in. He doesn't show much on the outside but he thinks a lot on the inside. He went away thinking about it and the decisions for him and for the others were easy in the end because they were making them in a group context. They all had the same interests.*
> *"They'd all talk to me and then they'd go away and talk about it together. That's how a relationship developed fairly quickly with all of them for me and then, through word of mouth, I had a lot of the other players coming in to see me as well including icons such as Michael Jones and Ian Jones. All the relationships created at this time have been enduring and very satisfying."*

One thing you never do is to describe DOJ as a player manager or agent. He won't wear that. Young players like me and the guys I had around me need direction in our lives. It's so easy to go off the rails when you're put in such a privileged position with good money coming in for playing rugby. And just because we reached a conclusion over the NZRU v WRC business, it didn't mean we were home and free. Again, I don't forget what DOJ told all of us then: "You guys are young and have good salaries. You've lived off the smell of an oily rag for a few years. If you want to get ahead now, then continue to live off the smell of an oily rag. Here's a book about property investment. Read it. You also need an accountant and a banker."

So, he rang Ralph Norris, who was with the ASB Bank then, telling him he had a group of players with money on their hands who all needed a banker. Ralph assigned a guy by the name of Peter Keenan to look after our interests. That's someone else I couldn't be more grateful for. It's the same thing with Grant McCurrach, who DOJ lined up as an accountant for us. Put together, this all provides a great support network giving my affairs some real order. Those relationships are so important to me and they've remained ever since. DOJ wasn't trying to live our lives for us, he was pointing us the right way to find out how to survive under our own steam.

> **DOJ:** *"They've all been smart. They've been prepared to take advice and to listen carefully and not waste their money on cell phones and fancy cars when they first started getting decent money. I told them they didn't need it, they needed something after rugby.*
> *"It was the beginning of my involvement in working alongside players, not as a manager. I don't like the description player manager. I'm trying to advise them. I'm their lawyer, not a manager or agent. I actually told them all from the start: 'You do not need a manager – there's only one guy in all of New Zealand who needs a manager and that's Jonah'."*

So my manager... sorry, lawyer... is central to succeeding as a professional rugby player but also in life beyond this game. We've become great friends through the years. I can tell him anything, approach him with any problem and I know he'll help and give me good advice. I don't see him as a lawyer. I see him as a good mate who's always there for me and looks after my best interests. I can call around to see him whenever I want. Basically he and his family are my Auckland family. That's how close we are. He's almost been like a de facto father. He's part of the family.

When Jodene and I got engaged I contacted Mum and Dad first but I also went around to see DOJ to let him know what I was up to, seeking his approval in a way. The same when we found out Jodene was expecting. We let our parents know and my next port of call was DOJ.

He has been huge for me with the deals he has set up for me and the directions he's steered me in. He's not there for the money, to take a big chunk of what I earn. He's not like those agents who are just there for their cut, 10 per cent or whatever it is of everything. He's just an awesome person. I'm lucky we met and I owe him so much.

Back when I first met him, he was in my ear about looking after my money. When I was just starting out and we had money coming our way as new professional players, he told me to invest in property. By the time I was 21, I was a homeowner, buying a place in St Johns. It was the best thing I ever bought.

These days my support network has grown to include another person DOJ introduced me to, Greg Dyer. Everything reached the stage where there was some order in my life, in the sense I owned property and could begin to look at other opportunities. DOJ was concerned that I have someone other than just an accountant, who could be more hands on in helping me look at business opportunities.

DOJ had met Greg through another one of his rugby clients, Mark "Sharky" Robinson. By coincidence Greg, who was friendly with Sharky, had expressed interest in getting involved in player management. That expression again!

> **DOJ:** *"I said to Greg: 'Don't think about being a player manager. With your skills there is a developing market to assist professional players in some of the business opportunities which they wish to pursue but don't have the experience or the time to pursue.' I mentioned that he might start with looking at some opportunities which Carlos wanted to explore at that time as well as my idea to bring on a website for Carlos. The rest is history now."*

Greg's been involved in some of my ventures, like setting up and running my website, merchandising and some business opportunities. More recently I've been interested in sorting out life after rugby, because I realise it's not going to last.

DOJ and I discussed those issues one day and then over a game of golf he introduced me to Greg. We had a good yarn and looked at a few options about directions I wanted to go in after rugby, or even before it ended actually, and to consider investment opportunities. One of the openings was buying an Esquires Coffee Houses franchise which we secured in a new business development on Auckland's waterfront (and opened in 2004).

We also looked into a couple of bars as possibilities. I was always interested in a bar but when you sit down with someone like Greg he goes over the whole plan with you, which is great. He gives you the good side and the bad side and the risk involved in investing in a business. Then I can make an informed decision.

While I've been a paid professional since 1996, I didn't even consider life outside and beyond rugby that much. I never wanted to think too far ahead but now I'm into the last three or four years of my career it has become far more important. It's a constant learn-

With Greg Dyer, who's done so much to help with my off-field business interests, including my venture into franchising with Esquires Coffee Houses.

ing process for me, though, and all the time DOJ is working with me with my so-called business interests which is actually a sideline for him.

> **DOJ:** *"One observation I have is that a lot of players weren't treated properly after the process they all went through to stay with the NZRU. The loyalty they showed in 1995 wasn't remembered in terms of the way they were treated. And it was ultimately that treatment that led Carlos to having such a serious look at going overseas."*

DOJ is right. It did lead to moments of real doubt further down the track but, when I signed to stay with the NZRU in 1995, I had few worries. New Zealand rugby was doing just fine by me then. It set up the pathway that would lead to the outbreak of pro rugby in 1996.

Obviously 1995 was a defining year for not just New Zealand rugby, but world rugby. That's when it changed forever. It also changed forever for me personally one day late in October when having a break from rugby was probably my main thought.

I had been reflecting on a season, my second since my move to Auckland, that had given me so much on the field and so much more experience off it as the NZRU and the WRC went at it with their own money game. I'd grown up an awful lot through that. On the field, the year had started with a shoulder problem forcing me out of Auckland's first three matches in the Super 10 but I'd had a great time playing for the New Zealand Colts in the Southern Hemisphere under-21 tournament in Argentina. Auckland had also won the Air New Zealand NPC yet again. We had some huge wins in that campaign, one of them 59-24 over Counties when I scored three tries. I couldn't complain about that.

So, the off-season was looking attractive along with watching some of the All Blacks' matches on their tour to Italy and France. A few of our boys were in the team, all of them in the forwards – Zinny and Robin Brooke, Richard Fromont, Craig Dowd, Olo Brown and Fitzy, of course.

In the very first match on tour, Andrew Mehrtens was injured playing against Italy A. I didn't think I was remotely close to being a contender for the All Blacks then. The selectors had named some standby players in the event of injury but I wasn't one of them. I didn't expect to be either.

When Mehrts was injured, some names were thrown around as possible replacements, two of them being Jon Preston and Stephen Bachop who had previously been All Blacks. One of those guys would have been a logical choice and I really didn't give it much thought at all.

At the time I was flatting with Junior in Sandringham but next thing I know, there's a phone call for me. I thought I was being had on but soon realised it was no wind-up at all – it was Murray Wright from the Auckland Rugby Union telling me I'd been called into the All Blacks as a replacement for Mehrtens on the tour. I rang Mum and Dad to let them know – they were rapt, as you'd expect – but I was still having trouble believing it. It's one of those incredible experiences. Me called up to join the All Blacks? Tell me again that it's true. There were media calls and interviews. It was all eye-opening stuff for a lad from Levin.

From then on it was just a blur packing and getting ready to fly out to France. It was no straightforward exercise meeting up with the team. I flew directly to France while they arrived from Italy but soon enough I found myself alongside my Auckland team-mates and all the others in the All Blacks. It was a really experienced unit then with guys like Frank Bunce, Jeff Wilson, Jonah, Walter Little, Josh Kronfeld, Ian Jones and Richard Loe just some of the others in the side. Suddenly they had this boy from Levin alongside them.

Auckland chief executive Murray Wright made a telephone call I'm never likely to forget.

I'd shifted to Auckland to develop my game and to strive to become an All Black one day but, after just two years there, I didn't necessarily I think I was ready for it right then. It was just a call-up really because Mehrts got injured – but heck, I was taking it.

By November 4 the All Blacks were playing Languedoc-Roussillon in Beziers and I was on the bench just taking it all in when I was given the call to replace Simon Culhane at halftime. I was buzzing, I know that, but that's about all I remember of it now apart from the fact Canterbury centre Tabai Mattson was also making his debut that day. He'd been travelling on the tour as a sponsor's representative when he was also brought in as a replacement to cover for injuries in the outside backs. We won the match 30-9 and that was my start as an All Black. I don't think I did that much actually.

I played the full game next time out a few days later when we – and I could say we now that I was an All Black – played in Bayonne. In a 47-20 win I kicked quite a few goals. For the first test in Toulouse, I was a dirty-dirty, in other words a spectator. It wasn't much fun either watching the guys being beaten 22-15.

Between the two tests, I had a second full outing against a French Selection in Nancy. It produced another big win – 55-17 – with a lot of goals as well before

The big guy Jonah (Lomu) . . . he was an unbelievable player at his best and a great guy. We'd come through the system together since secondary schools level.

I had the thrill of being selected as a reserve for the second test against France in Paris. That came about in a roundabout way through injury yet again. Jeff had been named at fullback and Ossie was on the bench, only Jeff failed a fitness test, Ossie was brought into his position and that left an opening on the reserves bench for me. Talk about things happening in a hurry. Just a few weeks earlier I had my feet up at home but now I was an All Black test reserve.

What a stadium that was – Parc des Princes – and what a time it was to be stripped for the possibility of making my test debut so soon. In the end, I didn't make it onto the field but the boys were outstanding in winning 37-12 ending a tour that was the start of my association with a lot of very good players. While I'd already been able to play alongside many of them for the Blues or Auckland it's something else again when you're in the All Blacks with them.

The other aspect was the chance to go to an exotic European country but that

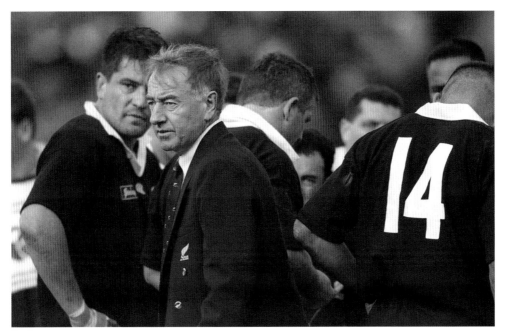

I spent so little time with Laurie Mains I never had a chance to find out too much about him as a coach. He didn't say much to me.

side of the experience was largely lost on me. It just flashed past and I can't really recall much of it at all, not even being in a city like Paris. All the sights are there but we weren't actually there all that long and besides I was just overwhelmed being an All Black on tour, never mind all the touristy bits that were around us.

I can't say Laurie Mains made much of an impact as a coach on me either. So much has been said and written about his methods and his personality. I have to say I can't add anything to the picture because I didn't have that much contact with him. He didn't have a lot to say to me. When I think about it, I don't think there was even a "well done" comment when I joined the tour. It was his farewell tour so a lot of players on that tour had had quite a bit to do with him for some time. They'd all been through a lot together, especially earlier in the year with the disappointment at the Rugby World Cup and then all the drama about the WRC and the business of whether the players would stay with the NZRU.

I was just the new boy and all I remember of Mains was him being a bit stern and detached. He wasn't known as Laughing Laurie for nothing I guess. I saw that side of him but as a fill-in player I never really had enough time to learn much about his ability as a coach and he wasn't going to be around the next year if I made the All Blacks again.

I'd made a start as an All Black but it was nothing like the way I'd imagine it might be. I was still a young guy really with a long way to go before I could feel I belonged.

John Hart was my first long-term All Black coach. I enjoyed him, too, although he did have a few too many meetings.

CHAPTER 7

Hart of the Matter

SO IT WAS VERY BRIEFLY hello Laurie, then just as quickly goodbye. That made way for what was one of the most significant years in rugby, some might say the most significant, because 1996 marked the year when all the rules changed. Now, after years of claiming to be amateur, the game came into the real world and players could be paid for playing the game.

It was also hello to John Hart, coming in to take over as All Black coach at a time when rugby would be going through some really big adjustments. It wasn't going to be easy and I guess there were a lot of people around who thought Harty, with his background in the corporate world, had good credentials to cope with this better than most.

This was such a huge year in all respects. The country's best players had the initial thrill of experiencing the world of Super 12 rugby, and that was certainly an exciting ride. For me that was very much what the first part of the season was about because I had no involvement in the All Blacks' home commitments against Western Samoa and Scotland or the early tests in another innovation, the Tri Nations Cup involving New Zealand, Australia and South Africa.

In the All Black trial, I sat on the bench but wasn't used and, instead of a specialist first five as a test reserve, Hart and the selectors went for Jon Preston's ability to cover both halfback and first five for those early internationals. It meant I didn't have an immediate chance to learn something of the way Hart operated as a coach and how the players handled the game's new age.

My opening came for New Zealand's eight-match tour of South Africa, the like of which there hasn't been again since professional rugby's debut season. Even then, this tour was a pale imitation of the great treks through history when All

Black teams would be in the republic for months on end rather than just a few weeks.

As far as tours go – and we don't really have them in true form anymore – this one on the veldt was just about as good as it gets. For all those years the All Blacks had been going to South Africa and had never won a test series; then along came pro rugby and it all happened at last.

There were four tests on consecutive weekends. One was part of the Tri Nations and the other three were a stand-alone test series while there were also four midweek games. It was a real test for pro rugby and how to go about it.

My role wasn't all that major but, with a huge number of 36 players required, I was able to make the cut for the trip. I was restricted to two appearances against Eastern Province and Western Transvaal in the midweek team captained by Taine Randell. Not a heavy workload but it was still a hell of an experience. Hart's theory on picking a tour party for this trip differed from tradition. On big tours, the practice had usually been to take 30 players with even coverage across all positions; shorter tours would normally have a reduced number of players, maybe 24-26. This had to be seen as a shorter one but the call was for 36 players, basically so there was a midweek team and a test team to run.

My first impressions of Hart were that he was a decent sort of a guy and I didn't have any problems with him as coach either. I couldn't find faults. It was really my first year in the All Blacks, apart from the brief taste in France, so in many ways I was still taking it all in. I didn't spend too much time analysing what was going on because there was just so much happening all at once. I was flat out worrying about doing my own job.

I was still only 20 and hadn't been exposed to too many coaches on what you'd call a long-term basis. Ted (Graham Henry) was the only one I'd had a reasonable amount to do with so I had someone to compare Hart with – and I soon found out he had a lot more to say than Ted. He talked a lot more and we had a lot more meetings as well. Maybe that was something to do with bringing a new All Black team together in his first year as coach. Maybe it was because rugby was in a new age and he thought a new approach was needed. Whatever it was, we certainly had longer meetings and a lot more of them than Ted ever had.

On occasions we were meeting two or three times a day. It reached the point where it felt like there were meetings for the sake of meetings. Harty must have thought he needed them because there were so many players to consider. Maybe it had something to do with his own corporate background and he carried it over into rugby. Every coach is different. They have their own ways.

Out on the training field, Harty liked to take control and was always talking. That doesn't always work because sometimes there's just too much to take in. With Graham Henry I would click into what he had to say far more than I did

Harty and Fitzy with the loot after we'd won a test series in South Africa for the first time in 1996.

with John Hart. I think that was because you didn't hear Henry as often as you heard Hart.

We had fantastic results on that tour, though, winning a series there for the first time which was obviously a great achievement. While I wasn't involved in the tests, it was still incredible to see the boys going out on four successive weekends against South Africa – on their soil – beating them in three straight tests, the first in Cape Town as our last match in the Tri Nations and then the next two in Durban and Pretoria to win the test series before losing the last in Johannesburg.

After effectively just starting out as an All Black in 1996, I suddenly found myself right in the middle of it in 1997. Until World Cup year in 2003, this was by far my busiest and most rewarding year in the All Black jersey.

The reason it was had a lot to do with Andrew Mehrtens. Not so much how he played, because he didn't. He was injured in the first home test of the year against Fiji which opened the way for Harty to give me my first test jersey. From being a basic All Black with a few tour appearances to my name, I became a fully fledged international making my debut against Argentina in Wellington – at the old Athletic Park – and then went on to play a total of seven tests during our home season.

Because it was my first, you'd imagine that match would register with me in some way. I can't say it does. Maybe I'm just different from a lot of other guys. I must be. It's a really big moment to play any test for your country and it meant

Halted but looking for support in the All Blacks' tour match against Emerging England in 1997.

so much to me to do so for the first time but detailed memories of the experience have long since gone. All I know is that I scored a couple of tries and kicked quite a few goals. What was it? Something like 33 points for the match. That's not important to me. What counted was playing in a test for the first time and winning it, and we won by plenty – 93-8 – so it was a bit of a cruise. Grizz Wyllie was coaching Argentina that day but we just had it all over them.

The second test in Hamilton was a bit closer – 62-10 – and again there were quite a few points in it for me with a try and few more goals. I'm sure Mehrts wasn't too pleased he was injured and missed the matches but I didn't mind coming into test rugby this way. In the end he was out for a bit of a stretch enabling me to start in the Bledisloe Cup test in Christchurch and the four Tri Nations Cup matches that followed.

It was a brilliant campaign as we went through unbeaten to retain both the Tri Nations title and the Bledisloe Cup. There was no question that John Hart was looking fairly special as a coach then.

The successes he was having probably explained why something else stayed the same – the endless meetings we had. They went on and on, so somehow we just had to get used to them. There were more ahead on the All Blacks' tour to Wales, Ireland and England, the last time the All Blacks have been on a tour of any real substance.

We had four tests, one each against Ireland and Wales and two against England but my involvement was limited to being on the bench once and making it on to the field in the 26-26 draw with the Poms at Twickenham. Of course, this was the tour when England got just a little bit excited despite us beating them 25-8 in the first test at Old Trafford.

We had Sean Fitzpatrick with us on that tour as captain but he barely made it onto the field because of his knee injury, the one that eventually ended his career.

We suffered through not being able to call on his leadership on that tour, especially in the Twickenham test when he was an important missing link. With him fit and on the field, I don't imagine we would have finished up with the draw which was greeted by the Poms like a win. They were way over the top after that result.

The match still held some interest for me because I went on in the last quarter and any chance to play at Twickenham was one not to be missed. This one was a bit different for me because I went on not at first five-eighth but replacing Walter Little at second five-eighth. I don't recall Harty saying he had plans to look at using me there but, with an injury to Walter, the opportunity presented itself. Any position would have suited me.

While there was concern in some areas about that result and the quality of the effort, I still hadn't detected anything then to indicate the All Blacks had lost any ground or that Hart was losing influence and effectiveness as the coach.

In some ways, that result came down to the performance of some individuals and the fact we'd reached the end of a long year. By then everyone was fairly keen to get home. At nine games, it was quite a long tour – a marathon by today's standards – and there's no doubt a lot of the guys were starting to think about being home in the sun.

On tour with All Black team-mates Tana (Umaga) and Ossie (Glen Osborne) . . . we all came into the side within a year or so of each other.

Whatever we thought about England's performances back then, history can now show it was around that time that they really began to develop as force building towards their World Cup win in 2003.

For one, Clive Woodward was there as coach and still had the job six years later; by then we were onto our third different coach from Hart to Wayne Smith and then John Mitchell. England's squad for those two tests showed Jason Leonard, Martin Johnson, Lawrence Dallaglio, Neil Back, Richard Hill, Kyran Bracken, Mike Catt, Will

Greenwood, Matt Dawson, Mark Regan, Danny Grewcock and Paul Grayson who were still in England's World Cup squad in 2003. Of our squad for that tour, Tana Umaga, Justin Marshall and I were the only ones still in the All Blacks six years later. Does that tell us something?

As it happened, England were the All Blacks' first opponents in the 1998 home season and my next test appearance – in the second test in Auckland – was also at second five. The Poms had come to New Zealand with a depleted side and were done over 64-22 as I sat and watched from the bench in Dunedin. But at Eden Park we weren't going at all well in the first half leading only 14-7 at halftime. Harty put me on for Mark Mayerhoffler at second five at the break and I ended up doing the goalkicking as well as we went on to win 40-10. It wasn't a flash effort, though.

And from there it turned into an ugly year, really ugly. We lost all four Tri Nations tests plus the third Bledisloe Cup match in Sydney, so allowing the Springboks to win the Tri Nations – which was a bit of a turn-up – and the Wallabies to regain the Bledisloe. My lot was nothing too special at all, starting in the 3-13 loss to South Africa in Wellington only to be replaced while I came off the bench myself twice. It wasn't a year to remember for anyone. What the season showed was how much we relied on a group of experienced guys who had quit since the 1997 Northern Hemisphere tour – Fitzy had lost his battle with his knee injury, Zinzan Brooke had retired and so had Frank Bunce. There as no question we felt their absence which made it a tough time for Taine Randell to come in as the new captain.

If it was a season best forgotten there was still nothing that stuck out to me about Hart being on shaky ground, not from my view from inside the team. I didn't have any concerns although I know he had to go through a bit of a process with the NZRU to keep the job for the World Cup year in 1999. As usual, I wasn't worried so much about what he was going through; I was just anxious to ensure I kept my place in the squad and made it to the World Cup. That was something I had some control over.

Whatever happened in 1998, I had nothing but confidence about our prospects in World Cup year in 1999. That might have seemed odd after the rough patch we'd gone through the previous season trying to adjust to life without Fitzy, Zinny and Frank. Any team would when you lose guys with so many tests behind them, more than 200 combined. By 1999 we were also without Michael Jones, Walter Little and Olo Brown so out went the experience of another 160-odd tests.

But I liked the exciting talent we had around and we still had a lot of experience in the shape of Jeff Wilson, Cully, Jonah, Mehrts, Justin Marshall, Josh Kronfeld, Robin Brooke, Ian Jones and Craig Dowd. That seemed to be a decent base to build a team around, especially with some of the new guys coming through.

One of the big problems for the 1999 Rugby World Cup was trying to find a home for everyone out wide. Apart from Jeff Wilson, we had Jonah (Lomu), Cully (Christian Cullen) and Tana (Umaga).

So I saw no reason why we couldn't be something that year, especially at the end when it would count at the World Cup. This was also a year that certainly had a hell of a start when Hart organised a boot camp for us in Auckland, the very famous boot camp. When we first got together for it I was asking myself: "What the hell are we doing this for?"

We started with a few drills and some swimming which all seemed reasonable enough but that night it started to turn. All we had for dinner was some soup and bread and then we were given a mattress about as thick as a few sheets of paper to sleep on in a big warehouse. I remember thinking: "Here we go!"

Here we go, alright. The next morning we were woken up at 4.00 and jumped on the back of some trucks with no idea where we were going. We finished up in the Woodhill Forest somewhere but at least we were given a decent breakfast of bacon and eggs. We soon found out we'd need it.

We were split into groups of six or seven and given a whole lot of tasks to perform. We had a soldier with us all the time to keep an eye on us but it didn't take long before we were all grumbling, swearing and getting more and more annoyed about this exercise.

One of our tasks was to take a power pole up a really steep hill, and I mean one of those big, solid power poles. Once we'd done that we had to dig a hole, put the pole in the ground and then someone had to sit on top of the pole without holding onto it and stay there.

We had other things to do as well and that night we had to sleep out. For food we had rations only. We could eat only when we really needed to. I think we had a tin of corned beef and some noodles for food. Our energy source was nothing more than sugar and water and our water supply was in a canister we had to lug around, which must have weighed around 50kg. Other than that we had just a piece of paper and a compass to help us get from point to point. This was a real test for us.

Big Jonah was in our group and we all had a turn as leader although all the decisions we made were always done on a team basis. At the time we were wondering what was going on and there were plenty of complaints. Gradually they disappeared and when I looked back on it later, I was glad I'd done it. A lot of people never experience anything like that but what we did would have been nothing to what the real professionals endure. We just had a couple of days of it where they have weeks on end of it.

By the end of it most of the guys were positive. The reward was the sense of achievement of doing something as a team unit. The physical part of what we had to do was sweet but a lot of the guys got grumpy for just one reason and that was the lack of food. No food was what killed me. I can never handle that for too long. It was a killer. Some of the guys lost 6kg even though we were away for only two days. It makes you stop to think about what the soldiers have to put up with when they're in the desert in Iraq or Afghanistan or somewhere like that.

While it was demanding, it was still sensible, nothing like the stupid drills the Springboks were forced to endure in their boot camp four years later before the 2003 World Cup. We didn't have to jump into freezing water in the nick like they had to. What we did was really demanding but it was realistic and it was also beneficial. I don't know what the South Africans were up to with that rubbish! That was really strange stuff.

Once past the boot camp and the Blues' Super 12 campaign, my involvement was only minimal for the All Blacks' home season, sitting on the bench for our first test against Manu Samoa before Tony Brown was given that job from then on. We were going well, too, regaining the Tri Nations Cup along the way but then having a night which raised some fears when the Wallabies retained the Bledisloe Cup by beating us 28-7 in Sydney. That wasn't pretty at all.

I guess one of the stand-out features of that year was Hart's use of Christian Cullen. Harty had decided Jeff Wilson should be the All Black fullback, which led

The decision to try Cully at centre at the 1999 Rugby World Cup wasn't a good one. He definitely belonged at fullback.

to Cully being pushed onto the right wing for the home tests and then for the Tri Nations Cup. That had to be seen as a waste of Cully's talents. He's much better-suited to fullback than the wing. And then, at the World Cup, Harty moved him to centre. I don't know what was going on then. He might have made a very good centre – if he'd had a lot more time playing there, but he hadn't. I don't think we ever saw enough of him playing at centre to warrant putting him in that role at the World Cup. I definitely would have persisted with him as the first-choice full-back. That's where he belonged. Whether the positional change hurt us at the

World Cup, I don't know. I'm sure it wasn't the reason why we lost to France in the semi-final. There were far bigger problems than him being at centre that night.

It had to be regarded as a selection gamble, first tried against Tonga in our opening game at the World Cup and used from then on, apart from the match against Italy when he was on the bench. I'm not sure how the players viewed Cully being played a centre because my involvement at the World Cup was over before it started. I went all the way there and never made it onto the field, heading home early after injuring my knee at training after the Tongan match. That was a huge disappointment and one I would take a while to fully recover from.

So my view of the tournament was essentially as a viewer like hundreds of thousands of other New Zealanders back home. I was laid up at home watching the bad news keep getting worse as the All Blacks' tournament ended in a dismal way. I wasn't there but I felt it just as badly.

That was the end of Hart but I never thought too much about that. It was the same as Mitchell four years later. When coaches come and go it's nothing to do with me. My general thought about coaches losing their jobs after defeats like that – Hart in 1999 and Mitchell in 2003 – is that it sucks to be honest. It's hard for a coach. I'm sure they all do their best to ensure everything is as right as it can be for every match. They certainly don't send a team out to fail.

The way I saw it watching the All Blacks lose to France at Twickenham in '99, a lot of players probably should have been fired that day as well. The coach can do only so much before a game and I'm sure Harty would have had them well-prepared but in the second half the All Blacks didn't look like they were there at all.

It's just so harsh for coaches because they nearly always cop the blame for the way players fail to perform. Like everyone else, I saw Jonah's try straight after half-time that took us out to a 24-10 lead and, when you're in a position like that, then surely the players are at fault for losing the match, not the coach. Hart was a coach with ability, still the only All Black coach to win a series in South Africa and, the way it's going with test series now rarely played, maybe it will stay that way. He was badly treated in my view.

Even worse was the reaction throughout the country to the All Blacks' failure to win the World Cup. It had become an obsession and, while the fans have a right to expect big things from the All Blacks, sometimes things go too far. They sure did in 1999.

The World Cup is important but it shouldn't be as important as some people make out. I want to win every test I play in or every Tri Nations Cup campaign. I don't just think about the World Cup.

I also like to see the strongest team playing as often as possible provided everyone's fit but I appreciate some players need to be rested from some tests these days because of the heavy demands on footballers at the top level.

Harty, assistant coach Wayne Smith and Doc (John Mayhew) . . . it was a year when our World Cup dream came to nothing again.

It's so much more challenging bringing in new All Blacks now. When I started out – and it's not that long ago – we still had things known as tours. There was my first one to France in 1995, another to South Africa in 1996 and then still another to Britain and Ireland in 1997. All of those tours had a reasonable number of matches giving coaches a decent opportunity to expose new guys to playing for the All Blacks.

Since then it has, with just a few exceptions, basically been wall-to-wall test matches only for the All Blacks. So, there isn't the chance to be eased into the All Black team the way I was. New players have to come straight into a test which, even though it might be against Fiji, Tonga or Italy is still a test and is treated that way. I feel sorry for young players now because of that.

At least when the John Hart era started, there were reasonable touring opportunities and maybe that's why we did so well in pro rugby's early days.

When Harty finished, the failure at the World Cup was what most people remembered but no one should ever forget what happened in South Africa in 1996. History won't.

I was sorry to see him go. It meant a major chapter in my All Black career was over and it would be the best part of three years before I could say I was well and truly back in black.

CHAPTER 8

A Man Named Jed

WHEN AUCKLAND RUGBY'S in good – or bad – shape, it usually follows that the Blues will reflect whatever the current state is. That's because the two are much the same, and that's not meant as a slight on other partners in the northern Super 12 franchise.

From time to time, those partners have changed. For the competition's first two years in 1996 and 1997 there were just two unions involved, Auckland and Counties Manukau, before Thames Valley was added in 1998. By 1999 the make-up had changed again as Auckland, North Harbour and Northland banded together.

Whichever partners the Blues had, though, Auckland obviously stood out as the dominant force, reflecting the size of the union and the successes generally enjoyed. Try the 1998 season as an example; then 20 of the 31 players in the Blues squad were from Auckland. The year before the split was 23 out of 33 and in the first year 22 out of 30.

In the original Super 12 mix in 1996 there were obviously huge benefits in the Blues inheriting the best of the best from Counties Manukau, and I'm naturally thinking of Jonah and Joeli. What a pair to have on the wings. Another plus, though, was having Counties Manukau coach Mac McCallion as assistant coach to Graham Henry.

Mac was a great character. He was a hard nut but he always knew how to have fun as well. Put it this way, he has never been scared of a beer. He was a good straight-up dude and I thought he and Ted worked really well together for the first three years of the Super 12 in 1996-97-98.

Left: It wasn't Jed Rowlands' fault, but it was strange making him Blues Super 12 coach in 1999.

Mac also had an impressive background in coaching generally, especially through his work with Counties, or Counties Manukau as the union became known. He took the Steelers into the Air New Zealand NPC first division final in both 1996 and 1997 while they were beaten in the semi-finals in 1995 and missed the last four by just one point in 1998. That's a decent record by any measure and plenty of coaches would like to say they owned one like it, because not many do. Of course, he also had a decent record as a player in his time.

With the knowledge he'd added to his coaching game working with Ted for three years, Mac would have been one of the best-qualified coaches in the country and surely should have been the man to replace Ted when he left for Wales. Maybe that was just too logical. Maybe not. Make that definitely not because the people who make these decisions believed Mac should stay as assistant coach in 1999. For the players, that was a strange move but what caught the attention even more was the choice made for our new head coach, a bloke by the name of Jed. From Taranaki, his full name was Jed Rowlands. And just like Jed Clampett in the old TV show *The Beverly Hillbillies*, Kiwi Jed must have thought he'd struck gold, rugby gold, that is. Even now, I'm not sure how it happened that he became a Super 12 coach. Odd things happen in rugby, like any sport, but this was way out there.

My usual way is not to get too wound up over coaching appointments. It's not my area of responsibility and I keep out of the politics. I'm just a player and I'll get on with things whoever the powers that be decide to make coach. They're the ones who make those calls and my attitude is usually one of what will be, will be – except with this one. Unusually, this was one I struggled with. First, because Mac wasn't given the chance we as players believed he deserved and, second, because we weren't confident Jed had the background for such a high-profile and high-pressure coaching position. That's not a criticism of Jed, just of the process which effectively discarded Mac despite his experience and achievements and gave Jed the top spot instead.

I wouldn't have had the slightest doubt that Mac would have been a decent head coach of the Blues. We all felt the same way after working with him for three years. He knew the players, he knew our structure and our strategies and, with the right man supporting him, as his assistant, it would have been a great way to continue the work he and Graham had done with the Blues. But I'm sure the bosses would admit they slipped up with this one. While it doesn't always work out right for a whole lot of reasons, this one was annoying because we had someone there who was suited for the position, only the people who do the thinking about these things thought it was a great idea to bring in a new head coach who was unknown to the Blues players and with no background at all in Super 12.

Jed seemed a nice enough guy to talk to, and clearly he was really intelligent, but those making the appointment should have known that these are not the key

We really felt for Mac (McCallion). We thought he should have replaced Ted as Blues coach.

credentials for a Super 12 coach. Headquarters obviously underestimated the importance of things like runs on the board, especially in Super 12, and the importance which players placed on the appointment of an established and respected coach.

Mac was a known quantity who was admired and rated by the players so we naturally wanted him to succeed Ted. Admittedly, we felt a strong loyalty and a bias towards Mac because we'd developed a relationship through working with him for three years. That meant it was never going to be an easy environment for Jed to come into, and it certainly proved very difficult for him. I didn't always appreciate it at the time but if I'm honest with myself now I guess we, as players, probably didn't do a lot to help him. I'm sure there are plenty of ways we could have given him an easier time by providing more support in various ways to enable him to settle into the position. With the benefit of hindsight, I think the other guys would agree with that but players can be really demanding (even a little precious) about the standards they expect and that's the way it played out back then. We'd been part of a successful environment and we all wanted to see those standards maintained.

Jed didn't have what you'd call loads of experience even at representative level. I knew he'd been Taranaki's coach in 1997 and 1998 although I couldn't remember ever coming across him. In fact, in both those years, Taranaki beat Auckland in the Air New Zealand NPC, first in New Plymouth and then in Auckland but on each occasion we were under-strength with a number of us on All Black duty in the Tri Nations Cup. Taranaki finished mid-table in '97 but did make the semifinals in '98 before being eliminated. You wouldn't have thought that was enough for HQ to throw someone into a Super 12 coach's job – but it happened. Mac was clearly annoyed, as anyone else would have been if they'd been assistant coach for three years and had then been passed over for the big job.

If we had some reservations from the outset, they were proven to be right when, in no time at all, the Blues went right off the rails. It was incredible that we could fade so quickly after being beaten finalists just a year earlier. A lot of that was to do with Ted going, as we saw with Auckland's poor performance in the NPC in 1998 after he'd left. The Super 12 collapse in 1999 was partly a continuation of the impact of his exit but, in my view, it had much more to do with the passing over of Mac and the effect that had on the morale of the players. They had so much confidence in him and, to be honest, were stunned by his non-selection as the coach. My personal feeling is that if he had been in charge we would have stood a decent chance of putting the show back on the right track. At the end of the day, though, it was still up to the players to win and do so with style. We failed ourselves and our fans. We have to accept that while the coach can have an effect on the team environment it's still up to the players to perform and not let the off-field issues interfere with performance. The coach can't go out and play, that's the players' responsibility.

While the players felt for Mac we admired him for biting his lip, staying on and trying to carry on – which, as we soon discovered, wasn't all that easy. We had no idea what to expect of Jed as a coach until we actually saw him at training for the first time, when our fears that he didn't have sufficient experience were soon proven correct.

Team morale wasn't helped by the fact Mac and Jed weren't getting on either. This probably wasn't all that unexpected after the way Mac had been overlooked, and was something which should have been foreseen. It couldn't have been comfortable for either of them. For his part, Jed must have felt awkward coming into a team such as the Blues and going over the head of a man who had the players' confidence and support. It reached the point where it seemed Jed and Mac didn't even talk to each other. The players saw that and we all thought: "What's going on here if the two coaches can't get on?" The mood that developed wasn't a good look and we probably all should have taken greater responsibility to prevent things falling apart.

The trouble was we found it difficult to accept Jed as a coach from the moment we first saw him in operation because he appeared to lack the knowledge and experience required at Super 12 level. And the further it went, the more we kept asking the same question among ourselves: "What were the decision-makers up to when they thought he could be the head coach of a Super 12 team, especially the Blues?"

It hits you fairly quickly when he turns up at training for the first time and says: "Stop doing spiral passes." That didn't help us warm to him really. If we wanted to develop a relationship with a new coach, it was going to be a challenge when he told experienced players to stop throwing spiral passes. To me, that just start-

Jed oversees a Blues training session. As players, we had trouble accepting him as a coach. Maybe we could have handled it better.

ed things off the wrong way.

As the weeks went by, the more we formed the opinion that this wasn't Jed's game, not at this level anyway. Maybe it would be later in his career when he'd gained more experience but right then, in 1999, it wasn't an ideal place for him to be in. He wasn't helped either by the fact that we'd lost a few players that season – most notably Jonah to the Chiefs – but, in the view of the players generally, Jed didn't seem to bring very much to the team in the way of a coaching style and game plan, not that I can recall.

You are always hearing about situations in rugby and other sports where a coach and his players don't get on through personality and style problems, or through a lack of respect between the two. In this case, it was the latter. The professional thing to do is to work out your differences or to try to work around the problem areas somehow. It's fair to say we didn't take that approach. We went the other way and removed ourselves. It's easy to realise now that we shouldn't have. We could have – and should have – been a lot more professional about it.

Faced with the situation with Jed, we got together as a team to talk about things and determined that we would try to guts it out, keeping it as positive as possible. All we could do was to try to win a game of rugby each week. We never went out there not caring what happened. But while it's still rugby and a game we loved to play, we also knew we were playing at a level well below where we should be if we were being properly coached.

Mac didn't have a lot to say at team meetings because of the feeling between him and Jed and I don't think Jed gave him much of an opportunity to speak either. Before we headed off to a match, Mac wasn't asked to say anything to us at all. Maybe he should have jumped in and just said: "Out of my way, I'm going to take this over." Possibly that would have created even more issues for him, though.

During the course of the season we had a few team meetings to talk through separately what was happening, a move led by the senior players. It was tough on new players to see the Super 12 working this way at the Blues because professional rugby shouldn't operate that way. Then again, we felt we didn't have any real choices although I know I would approach things differently in future. That's the benefit of experience I suppose.

History shows we had other ideas in 1999. We ended up deciding that we wouldn't really pay much attention to Jed at all and we even considered the possibility of doing our own thing, basically coaching ourselves. It didn't quite play out that way, which was just as well, but it was close. That's how bad it was in our eyes and I'm sure Jed felt the pressure we created. It's the only time in my rugby career when I've felt so strongly about a coach. It's also the only time when I've had coaches who didn't speak to each other.

Our results and the type of rugby we played throughout that season provided all the evidence needed that something was-n't right inside the Blues. In the first three years of the competition we'd won 32 of our 39 matches, drawing one and losing only six with an average winning score of something like 37-27. Suddenly, we were down to win-ning just four games, drawing one and losing six. We were never flogged by any side but we never belted any team in those few wins we had. We were just mediocre, nothing bet-ter. That was a statement of the obvious. We scored only 202 points in 11 matches, only 18 on average a match, while we could count only 15 tries in the entire campaign. That didn't add up after we'd been such an attack-ing force the previous three years.

We had a period where we managed some success, following up losses to the Highlanders and the Crusaders with a draw against the Reds and then four wins on end over the Chiefs, the Waratahs, the

Two men who lifted Auckland rugby back to the top after some rough times . . . new coach Wayne Pivac (left) and assistant Grant Fox.

Hurricanes and the Cats but a season I couldn't wait to end then hit a run of four defeats by the Sharks (6-12), the Stormers (23-37), the Bulls (19-21) and the Brumbies (16-22). By the end of the programme, I wasn't even at first five any-more, with Northland's Tony Monaghan in the No 10 jersey while I ran at sec-ond five. It was just a rough ride.

On reflection, if Jed was to be involved, the common-sense decision would have been to bring him in as assistant coach to Mac so he could get the Super 12 coaching experience he lacked and form good relationships with players without the pressure of being head coach. It was certainly a choice out of leftfield. Everyone thought so then and everyone knows so after the event. Unfortunately it meant things were always likely to go wrong. It really didn't add up that head-quarters would take such a gamble with the most successful franchise in the Super 12 at that stage, setting us back a long way as we went from winning the Super 12 the first two years and then being beaten in the final in 1998, to finishing as low as ninth in 1999. That was an enormous fall from grace.

The end of the Super 12 campaign wasn't the end of the problem as far as the Auckland Rugby Union was concerned as Jed had also been appointed to coach Auckland that year in the Air New Zealand NPC. The ARU obviously recog-nised the depth of the problem facing it and stepped in to make a change by

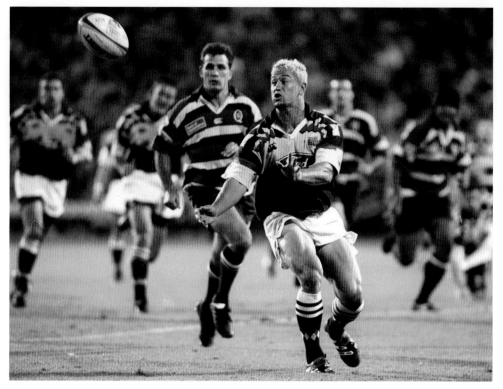

The Blues' jersey has changed a lot, so have the hairstyles. For a while I was a blond-haired Maori boy from Horowhenua.

appointing Wayne Pivac as the new coach with Grant Fox assisting him. That was a real relief for the Auckland boys. What a difference that was after the Super 12.

Because they were brought in late, it was a testing assignment for Wayne and Foxy, even more so because of the state of Auckland and Blues rugby at the time. And with the Rugby World Cup looming, they would have limited access to the All Black players in the Auckland squad (Andrew Blowers, Robin Brooke, Dylan Mika, Craig Dowd and me).

I was lucky enough to play in Auckland's first four matches before joining the World Cup squad. We gave Wellington a real touch-up 45-6, Northland were beaten 31-6, we battled against North Harbour (23-16) and then had a big win over Southland (35-7) as well. The boys were just beaten by Canterbury but then went all the way to cause a real shock by taking the title, beating Wellington 24-18 in the final. It was a great achievement by Pivac and Fox in their first campaign. I was so rapt for them and for the players. By then I was back home, my World Cup over before it started after injuring my knee, but it was still a real boost seeing Auckland win that one after what we'd been through in the past year.

And, no, Foxy didn't mind me throwing spiral passes in the games I was able to play.

CHAPTER 9

Leicester Calling

AFTER THE JED ROWLANDS EXPERIMENT, the Blues were faced with a long road back to where we'd been. There wouldn't be any quick-fix way of getting there either but if there was some repair work to be done I wasn't going to be much use trying to help as the new millennium arrived. Instead I faced a bit of a mission myself recovering from knee surgery after my injury at the 1999 Rugby World Cup.

The frustration of not being able to play didn't help and one way or another it was fair to say I was at a bit of a low in 2000, and that's not like me. There were reasons why I could so easily have said no more to New Zealand rugby as the year unfolded. There was a bit of discontent, you could say.

At the Blues we were having a shot at beginning a new era after a very short one with Jed. This time HQ had given us a coaching team of Gordon Hunter as the top man and Frank Oliver as his assistant. Once again, there was no association with our part of the country in either man but Gordy had a damned good coaching record with Otago and the Highlanders as well as working with John Hart as an All Black assistant coach and selector.

He was a good man, well respected. His eye was fairly evil but he was great to have around and someone I knew through the All Blacks. He'd tell so many police stories from his days as a detective. Whether half of them were true, I don't know, but he was always good to listen to. Frank was fairly straight-up, a lot like Mac McCallion in many respects but Mac was probably better-suited to our team. And completing the new-look structure, we had JK (John Kirwan) in as our manager. He was good for that role in the sense of being a past player although he had no real experience for it.

The fact we had Gordy and Frank coaching us probably summed up the picture in New Zealand rugby, or more accurately Auckland rugby. There was a bit of a problem finding coaches for all the teams around that time. Ideally, it helps to have your coaching staff from the area the franchise covers rather than bringing them in from outside (like Hunter and Oliver) but there just weren't genuine local contenders at the time. There didn't seem to be anyway.

There was some improvement under Gordy and Frank in the Super 12 that year but it was going to require a lot more to regain the ground lost in 1999. We were also into a heavy rebuilding period with a lot of really good players moving aside in the previous couple of years. For all that, we had a reasonable year with wins over the Brumbies, Waratahs, Hurricanes, Highlanders, Northern Bulls and Sharks for six wins and five losses, just two points off fourth place to finish sixth.

I'd started the year slowly recovering from surgery on my knee, playing only five Super 12 games and failing to find a place in the All Black squad. Wayne Smith was now in charge after John Hart had quit but I couldn't blame anyone but myself for not being selected. It came down to form. I was coming back from my knee injury and it took me a while to get back into the swing. I had months of rehabilitation after the operation and I was always going to be late beginning that season. I was told I'd be out for six months but it wasn't quite that long in the end. When I did return to play for the Blues, I didn't think my form was there to warrant All Black selection for the home tests against Tonga and Scotland or the Tri Nations Cup matches. I was still getting over my operation, gradually building back to where I wanted to be with Tony Brown around then as the back-up to Andrew Mehrtens.

> **DOJ:** *"Carlos had the operation on his knee and he couldn't play much Super 12 in 2000. The Blues weren't winning and everyone was saying: 'Why hasn't Carlos won us the game?' Junior Tonu'u had gone so he didn't have his long pass anymore and he didn't have a dominant forward pack in front of him and people were bagging him."*

There was a bit of a confidence issue when I returned in what turned out to be a difficult year. My first game back for the Blues was off the bench against the Stormers and then I played in the next four matches but I wasn't at what I regarded as my best.

It was also contract time for me and that's where the problems began. I was in the last year of a three-year NZRU contract and I'd have to say I was interested in the chance then of playing in England following an approach made by Leicester. I had an initial conversation with Dean Richards, then Leicester's coach, who had come out to New Zealand early in the year to talk to a small number of

Meeting up with Leicester's coach Dean Richards on a trip DOJ (David Jones) and I made to England and Scotland in 2000.

players. We kept the NZRU in the loop on the negotiations with Leicester because it had a right of first refusal on any overseas offer. Despite that, there was a bit of bad feeling around about it. Wayne Smith had a few words with DOJ which wasn't particularly encouraging and, along with my gradual recovery from surgery, I was feeling a bit disheartened to the point I could quite easily have said no more to New Zealand when the Leicester deal was all on.

Whether the discussions with Leicester were held against me when the All Black squad was selected, I don't know. I was available and had recovered although I was still the first to admit I wasn't playing at the level I expected of myself.

DOJ: *"Carlos was disheartened at the apparent disinterest from the All Black selectors. He had the same feeling when John Mitchell came on board and said he wasn't a first five, that he was a fullback. Ironically, at both times when the All Black selectors showed indifference to him, overseas interest was at its strongest. At these times we seemed to have a rush of clubs approaching him. They were just gleeful at the possible opportunity of signing Carlos.*

"The public criticism of Carlos and the selectors' indifference to him was the trigger for the interest in going overseas. Northern Hemisphere observers were puzzled by New Zealand commentators' criticism of a player they rated as a genius – and this from countries we like to say don't appreciate 'flair'. New Zealanders don't celebrate

having a player like Carlos in the way the English and, in particular, the French do. We need Carlos Spencers in the game but if we keep bagging players like him, no young player will want to emulate him. It's going to frighten young people and it will also mean coaches won't pick players like him because they, too, will be frightened of the criticism. It's a vicious circle."

It reached the stage where I signed a deal with Leicester which was subject to a number of conditions. One was that the NZRU didn't exercise their right of first refusal on me. So, we sent a letter to the NZRU laying out the terms of the contract we had been offered by Leicester subject to the NZRU not exercising their right of first refusal.

DOJ: *"That was in early to mid April. I asked them to please let me know what their view was on first right of refusal. There was… silence… silence… silence. Will you please give us a response? Silence… silence. In fact, it wasn't until nearly the end of May that we had a response."*

It came to a head when I had been invited to play for the Barbarians in a few games in the United Kingdom but I couldn't. The Barbarians asked whether I would like to come with DOJ anyway to see the Barbarians play. Leicester said they'd pay for me to travel so I could have a look at the club and their set-up at the same time.

At the time I was doing my rehab on my knee, which prevented me playing for the Barbarians. We told the NZRU we were going to make the trip which also involved going to see the Barbarians play Scotland at Murrayfield but I would have been back in plenty of time for All Black commitments if I was required.

DOJ: *"It was just a few days before the All Blacks were going to be named – on May 28 – that the NZRU responded about the right of first refusal. Carlos and I were leaving for England just before the team was named. It was suggested to me by the NZRU that the All Black selectors might see Carlos as an integral part of the World Cup team moving forward for 2003, but, with the All Blacks being named on Sunday, it was unlikely Carlos would be selected if he hadn't been re-contracted.*

"The next morning, the day before leaving, I got a letter from David Rutherford, CEO of the NZRU, stating among other things that the NZRU reserved all its rights in the event Carlos does default in his obligations under the contract (legal-speak for: 'Carlos could risk his contract being cancelled if he went up to the Barbarians' matches'). Strange that – on the one hand a warning that his contract could be cancelled, on the other a desire to re-sign him to 2003."

Top: Gleneagles, where the Barbarians stayed in 2000 . . . DOJ is in the middle with Joeli (Vidiri)
there with us. Below: I'd played at Twickenham before, now I was a spectator to watch a club final.

Well, we went on that trip and, if I breached my contract by doing so, I was never told about it. The trip was great. I loved it. It was good to get away from what was going down over the contract business, which I really didn't need but it was an example of how difficult it has been dealing with the NZRU over contractual matters.

We were away only about a week or 10 days during which time the All Black team was named with Todd Blackadder as the new captain. My name wasn't anywhere to be seen.

Thousands of kilometres away we visited Leicester and Gleneagles before DOJ had to go home a few days early. Leicester had a good set-up and we saw Peter Wheeler, the boss there, as well as meeting a number of the guys like Martin Johnson and Neil Back. We had a good look around and also checked out the Barbarians club. After that we went by train to Scotland and Gleneagles where the Barbarians were staying and watched the game at Murrayfield.

DOJ: *"When we were back in New Zealand, some people were putting a bit of pressure on Carlos saying that I was driving Carlos to leave New Zealand, which was never the case. All I was doing was helping to put options in front of him to consider. As it turned out, subsequent to this we were able to do a deal where the NZRU exercised their right of first refusal but it was a really long process."*

I know I could easily have gone to Leicester. The proposition had a lot going for it but in the end my decision was taken out of my hands when the NZRU decided to take up their right of first refusal on my contract. I was signed up until the end of 2003 so I could continue to be a part of the Blues and Auckland and also to strive to make it back into the All Blacks. For the home season and the Tri Nations I had nothing to do with Smith's first season as All Black coach so I could only watch as the guys came out of the Tri Nations in second place with two wins and two losses.

For me, the Air New Zealand NPC was a vital outlet if I was to win favour with the new All Black set-up. I felt happier about myself, regaining the confidence that had been missing earlier in the season as I played every one of our 10 matches. This time I was also able to get a better line on the way Wayne Pivac and Grant Fox operated after a brief glimpse of them in 1999.

They were certainly proving to be a quality combination, two of the best coaches I've seen working together. That's not always easy, getting the chemistry and balance right between coaches but these guys had it worked out. Pivac impressed a lot while Foxy was so thorough, definitely the more serious and intense of the two. He needed to relax a bit more a lot of the time and he learned to do that.

Playing spectator again . . . this time we were watching from one end of Murrayfield when the Barbarians met Scotland.

Our campaign didn't work out as well as it had a year earlier, losing to Canterbury in regulation play to finish second behind them, so earning a home semi-final, which should have been good for us. This time it wasn't. Wellington came north and hammered us 48-23 with Christian Cullen, Jonah Lomu and Tana Umaga all on the score sheet. Ugly, very ugly.

But the run in the NPC did help me back into the All Blacks for the short end of year tour to France and Italy for what proved to be the only time I played for New Zealand in the time Smith was the All Black coach. My involvement included a few minutes on the field as a replacement when we won the first test 39-26 in Paris, filling in at second five for Daryl Gibson outside Andrew Mehrtens, while I was given the first five's job for the test against the Italians in Genoa, a match we won 56-19.

That was one of the few times I had the job ahead of Mehrts but it wouldn't be until 2003 that I had a really prolonged crack at the role. There's never been any rivalry between us despite what people might believe. I've got a lot of respect for Mehrts. He's done the country proud every time he's been in there. He's a great player and I've never ever thought or said I should be there instead of him.

So many people believe there's some sort of rivalry between Mehrts (Andrew Mehrtens) and me. I've got so much respect for him.

It's really only been a media thing to me. I would think Mehrts would say the same thing. Whenever either of us had the chance, we went out there and did our own job.

I didn't know it then, but that appearance in Genoa was going to be my last in the All Black jersey for just on two years. It meant my experience of All Black life with Smith as coach was very limited, a bit like the time I had with Laurie Mains on my very first tour to France five years earlier. What did I see in Smith then? He was a very technical coach. He was a good back coach and had obviously done

Another game, another team and a new position . . . scoring one of two tries when playing fullback for the New Zealand Maori against Australia in 2001.

it all before. But, strangely, there was never any time we sat down and talked about first five's play, given the fact he had played there in his time.

As it panned out, he lost the job within 12 months when he indicated he wasn't sure whether he wanted to continue. The position was advertised, he reapplied and he failed to succeed. That was a fairly odd business I guess but it didn't really interest me one way or the other. I didn't have any view on whether he should have had another go.

By the time the 2001 season came around, my football focus had nothing to do with the All Blacks, not through choice. The year the Blues had didn't help at all. Our stocks slumped lower than ever when we came 11th in a 12-team race. Even Jed Rowlands' year wasn't that bad when we'd finished ninth.

It was a really challenging year for another reason, too. Gordon Hunter had been suffering dreadfully from cancer in 2000, courageously staying involved for as long as he could but ultimately he couldn't continue. Gordy was just one top bloke and everyone who'd been involved with him through the All Blacks, Otago, the Highlanders and the Blues – not to mention services teams – couldn't rate him highly enough. He was only 52 when he died on March 9, 2002.

In the shuffle to our coaching structure for the 2001 Super 12, Frank Oliver became the top man, JK moved from manager to become assistant coach and Sean Fitzpatrick took the manager's job. We had three proven All Blacks in the positions of control but, for a whole lot of reasons, the mix had something missing. Let's just say, it didn't work out too well for everyone concerned including me personally, proof positive that the recovery process from the 1999 woes would be a slow one for the team.

I did have an outlet to perk me up, though. As I was out of the All Black frame, I was able to become reacquainted with the New Zealand Maori in a mini campaign comprising a match against the Wallabies in Sydney and another against Argentina in Rotorua. There was a big change as well – I was picked at fullback. Not necessarily my preference but I wasn't against it either and I relished the chance to attack, especially against Australia when I grabbed our only two tries when we were beaten 41-29. That was a good tune-up for the Aussies before their three-test series against the Lions, a campaign they went on to win. A couple of weeks later we accounted for the Pumas, winning 43-24, no tries from fullback that time but quite a few goals.

I tell you, though, it was fun being back with the bros. Against the Wallabies, we had Bruce Reihana on one wing, Caleb Ralph and Daryl Gibson in the midfield, Rhys Duggan at halfback, Taine Randell and Troy Flavell as the flankers, Mark Cooksley and Norm Maxwell the locks, Greg Feek one of the props and Norm Hewitt at hooker plus me in No 15. In other words, 11 of the starting players were All Blacks with the only exceptions being Roger Randle – and he became an All Black at the end of the year – Glen Jackson, Deon Muir and Deacon Manu. The Maori have such a refreshing attitude to playing the game. It really picks you up.

That ended up being the high point of the year in some respects because Auckland didn't function so well in the NPC either, trounced 38-10 when we challenged Canterbury for the Ranfurly Shield – my friends in Christchurch loved that – and then we were back for more of the same in our NPC semi-final. What a nightmare that was. Canterbury at Jade Stadium twice within a couple of weeks and the second time we were bashed up 53-22. I could comfortably say I'd had better years than both 2000 and 2001 in my rugby career – and there was still a lot worse to come. That's the way it goes sometimes. Sport does that to you.

CHAPTER 10

Disenchantment

ANYONE WHO KNOWS ME is well aware I'm not a dummy-spitter by nature. Not in public, at least. It's in my make-up to let things lie and just shift on to the next base. There's not much point getting worked up about things you can't do anything about.

But it's not as easy to handle when your pride, professional pride, suffers. Maybe it was those two games I played for New Zealand Maori in 2001. That's all I could think. In all the years I'd been playing rugby at top level just a few matches had been at second five or fullback, even a game at centre when I toured South Africa as an 18-year-old with the Maori in 1994.

I haven't done the maths but by the end of the 2001 home season I'd had a fair few matches at first five. That much was obvious, only the time had arrived when I was evidently no longer considered a first five. As I say, I have never quite figured out how this came to pass but I need to go back to late in the 2001 season to look at how it developed.

It was then that John Mitchell was appointed coach ahead of Wayne Smith. I didn't take too much notice other than realising there'd been a change and it didn't worry me in any great way – but when Mitchell and the selectors picked a 30-man side to tour Ireland, Scotland and Argentina my mood changed a bit.

There were two first fives picked and I wasn't one of them. Mehrts was obvious but not quite so obvious to most people was the choice of Waikato's David Hill. I don't mind admitting I was disappointed when I missed that team because injury wasn't a factor. I was available.

Hill was a fairly "interesting" selection I guess. Mitchell obviously thought he could do the job and went for him. That's the decision. I don't stay down for

John Mitchell arrived as All Black coach and said he didn't think I was a first five. I can't say I thought too much of him when he said that.

long. It doesn't help sitting around being shitty about it. They didn't pick me for that tour and there wasn't a lot I could do about it other than give them no reason to do it again when the new season started.

Auckland didn't have a great time in the NPC in 2001, finishing poorly in the NPC semi-finals. It was a poor year for the Blues as well but I don't blame team form for missing out on All Black selections. It comes down to me alone.

I had one call from Mitchell that I remember when he told me I wasn't in that team. That was all. At least he did call. But the one thing I wasn't impressed with from Mitchell was when he came out publicly saying I wasn't a first five, I was a fullback. That's how he saw me. I didn't think much of him when he said that. He didn't talk to me directly about that, he just came out with it in the media and

I didn't know what to make of it. It seemed fairly strange to me.

John Hart had tried to use me at second five a few times so Mehrts and I were both on the field. I didn't mind that so much. That had the potential to work quite well because we had the chance to line up on either side of attacking scrums when we had a good-sized blindside or at other times in broken play. There were some variations you could work on.

I wouldn't see myself as a fullback as my first preference but I could probably play there. I'd had a few appearances there over the years, only a few.

DOJ: *"When Mitchell said Carlos wasn't a first five and that he should concentrate on fullback, it's the only time I have seen Carlos really disenchanted. He was quite hurt by what Mitchell had said, not so much by the non-selection but being told he should concentrate on being a fullback, which meant he was being told he wasn't a first five's elbow.*

"The English and French could not believe Carlos hadn't been selected so clubs from both countries immediately contacted me and said they'd like to have Carlos. They were stunned – but elated – that the All Blacks didn't want him. They thought it was a chance to get Carlos because they knew he would be disillusioned. They were so keen to have him they were prepared to pay him more than they'd pay for any other top All Black at that time and Carlos wasn't even a selected All Black. They were also prepared to pay him two years in advance of his contract finishing and to pay him a substantial deposit up front. That's the only player that's ever happened to that I've been involved with.

"An agent from Perpignan came out from France to see me at the beach in the Christmas holidays and Carlos was so disillusioned he was prepared to consider it. He didn't commit in the end but he was under threat throughout that year."

I kept my head, did a bit of deep breathing over the summer and tried to freshen up for the 2002 season. I succeeded but I wasn't out of the fullback frame by a long stretch. I found that out playing for the Blues, New Zealand Maori and Auckland.

The Blues showed more changes for the fourth year running but maybe, just maybe, there were signs of settling down just a little at last. Fitzy was still the manager but now we had Peter Sloane as coach and Foxy as assistant coach. We muddled through to finish a fairly distant sixth with six wins and five losses. It had to be viewed as a pass mark and a move in the right direction at last.

For me personally it was a season where the national selectors – or Mitchell at least – saw me as a fullback and it was no accident that I wore the No 15 jersey five times for the Blues while I was at first five the other six games. I was coming and going a bit but did the best I could.

I wasn't able to do enough to attract the selectors when they settled on their All Black squad for the home tests and the Tri Nations but, for the second season running, that meant another trip with my cuzzies. This time the Maori had a four-match tour with games against Queensland, New South Wales, Australia and the New Zealand Barbarians. It wasn't a bad tiki tour because it took us all the way to Perth for the clash against the Wallabies. This time we didn't have as much All Black power but we still put a lot of heat on Australia before being beaten 27-23. Again I had a taste of playing at fullback but just the once against Queensland.

There was more of it to come playing for Auckland in the Air New Zealand NPC but this was still very much the making of the year for us for one highly significant reason. Providing real impetus for our cause was Graham Henry who had returned home from Wales, initially accepting a background role helping Wayne Pivac and Foxy with the Auckland team. He went on to fill a similar role for Peter Sloane and Bruce Robertson with the Blues in the 2003 Super 12 and again with Auckland in the NPC in 2003.

What he basically did was all the video work, all the analysing of the opposition in defence. When he wanted to talk to the players about his side of the operation he did. He wasn't involved directly in the preparation of the sides but he was always around. He might talk to individuals here and there or have something to say in a team meeting when we were together but, other than that, he was there mainly for defence and providing analysis.

Obviously in coming into that role he knew he probably couldn't have too much to say because Wayne and Foxy were still the coaches at Auckland, Sloane and Robertson at the Blues so he couldn't step out of line and get too involved. He had to be careful really. He respected them and the chance he'd been given on coming home. He's not one to come in and try to start running the show, which was good. He did what he had to and it was great. He was so helpful. Everyone involved would tell you how grateful they were to have him around and what he did for the side.

Graham came along at the right time. A lot of people think he was the main reason why the Blues and Auckland started winning. What I'd say is that he helped us a lot, a hell of a lot, but plenty of signs had been there before. We had a tough period for a while but all the time new players were coming along and were becoming more and more experienced. We had talent. It just had to be developed. Graham gave us greater organisation on defence.

In the years after Graham left for Wales, we had fallen away a lot with both Auckland and the Blues. We didn't have a great structure in place and we probably weren't a great side either on the field or off it, not as close as we have been the last couple of years. There were a whole lot of little things not right and they all added up to create an environment and a team that wasn't right. Bringing

Graham and Raewyn Henry . . . it was a huge benefit to Auckland and the Blues when Ted came back home and worked with us in a background role.

a team together off the field is also another one of Graham's strengths. He does that very well.

He's a person who has a real presence. He's one of those people who when he says something you listen. You know that when he talks it's going to be worthwhile. He's not one of those coaches or people who will say something just for the sake of it

You look at him and he's a very assured person, not cocky, just assured and comfortable in what he's doing. It rubs off on us. We feel good around him. You never feel nervous or uncertain when you have him around.

He finished up doing two NPC campaigns in an adviser's role. Both times we won, too, doing so in 2003 without the World Cup All Blacks. Not just that, but taking the Ranfurly Shield off Canterbury as well. I think he would have done the same thing again if that's how things worked out. Whether he would have been totally happy about it, I don't know. I'm sure there were other jobs that might have interested him more but he would have carried on just the same because that's the passion he has for rugby. As it was Wayne and Foxy decided to finish up and Graham was initially appointed Auckland's 2004 NPC coach, before that was overtaken by an even more important calling – coaching the All Blacks.

But Ted was incredibly enthusiastic in the work he did with Auckland when he came home from Wales. He's not always well read by some people, especially the British media but that's the Poms for you. They look at him and think he can be a bit scratchy and moody. They just don't know him properly or don't want to understand him.

With Ted in the mix, we had a brilliant time in the 2002 NPC. We had losses to Taranaki, Canterbury and Waikato so we weren't necessarily so favoured to make it through in our semi-final, especially because we were heading back to Jade Stadium where we'd had two shocking results on our previous two visits in 2001. My friends down there weren't so chirpy this time as we won 29-23 to set up a final against Waikato in Hamilton.

Again the odds-setters saw this match one way and it wasn't ours. So much for that, because we had a stunning night running in six tries to win 40-28. By then I was back at first five – I played there in the last four games – but my other six appearances were all at fullback in accordance with certain people's wishes.

Moving back to No 10 was naturally more comfortable for me and helped to push me back into All Black contention for the end of year tour to England, France and Wales. Maybe my style of game counted against me sometimes in selection discussions. There was always talk around that it did but I couldn't say. I wasn't going to change, though. I wouldn't change the way I play for anyone. This is the way I am and if I'm wanted as that type of player for the Blues, Auckland or the All Blacks, that's brilliant. I wouldn't change even if it meant it was the only way I could get into the All Blacks.

I've enjoyed approaching the game this way and I'd never want to play any other way. I want to be happy playing football and that way is the way I've grown up expressing myself. I wouldn't enjoy it any other way. Ten-man rugby isn't for me. I accept you need to adopt that approach from time to time in some games and some situations within a game. There might even be a whole game you need to play that way – although even then I'd want to chuck a bit of the flamboyant in there somewhere!

Most of what I do is unplanned. It happens on the basis of what I see in front of me. You can't plan a lot of what I do. You can have a game plan, yes. But most of what I do is on the spur of the moment, instinctive stuff. The no-look passes? They just happen. If I go one way, a defender comes with me and I know that's created a hole on the other side, the expectation is someone will be running at that hole and I'll flick out one of those blind or no-look passes. I'll have a look just before I get the ball and will see something is possible. Then I'll go for it. It

My real thrill playing rugby is to work with the ball. Expressing myself is the way I've grown up playing the game and I wouldn't want to change it.

can't be planned two or three phases out.

I usually say to the other guys to expect the ball when I have it because something might happen at any time. I don't know myself because I can't predict what will happen and when but anything's possible. The players know me now, they know the things I might do. Expect the unexpected is probably the way we operate.

It's different with the kicks but even then they're usually planned only one phase out with a nudge, a wink or a call. Quite a few times Dougy (Howlett) will give me a call. He sees a lot of things that could be on. He's one player with good vision but a lot of today's players aren't brought up that way. There's a lot of robotic rugby that goes on in a lot of places now.

I can only guess it was the way I played as a first five that encouraged Mitchell and his selectors to recall me for the tour in 2002 although I don't recall any discussion with Mitch about it. All I remember is the comment about me being a fullback. And I would remember that, wouldn't I? The first contact we had was when we came together as a team for the tour. The side was stacked full of new All Blacks after a whole lot of players – especially Canterbury ones – were left at home.

Obviously something changed in his thinking but I have no idea when or why. He never spoke to me but suddenly I was in the All Black touring team as a first five. As fate would have it, I was even picked to start the big test of the three against England at Twickenham on November 9 – and the last time I'd worn the jersey had been November 25, 2001. To say it was good to be back in black wasn't close to how I felt. Unfortunately, I lasted only half the game before a shoulder injury forced me out of the game with Mehrts coming on to replace me.

We had a lot of new faces in that team, and a lot of so-called first-choice All Blacks were left at home, but I still didn't see it as being an under-strength All Black side. There was nothing wrong with that team, it was strong. We still should have won that test but we made a few silly errors and let them in for a couple of tries that ended up killing us.

Mitchell seemed alright to deal with on tour. Working together with Robbie Deans, Mitch wasn't a lot different from a lot of other coaches. There was plenty of talk around that Robbie tended to run the football side of things and that was certainly the case. He came up with most of the ideas about the way we would play, just about everything actually. There was some thought Mitch was more of a manager type, like you see in English soccer, but that wasn't the case. He operated very much as a coach and Deans was the assistant.

One way or another, Mitch came in for a lot of comment. Some of it we knew about, some we didn't. I know some people on the outside weren't necessarily too impressed to see an All Black coach running with the players the way he did. Their view was that he should be a little more at arm's length from the players,

By the end of 2002 I was back in the All Black frame for the tour to England, France and Wales. Mitch saw me as a first five by then.

not running around with his shirt off. I can't speak for the other boys in the team, but that didn't bother me. He really only got involved when we were in game situations or just mucking around. When the serious stuff was happening and we were concentrating on some aspect of the game, then he stayed out of it. If he wanted to get in there and muck around with the boys, then I thought good on him. It didn't happen with John Hart and it won't happen with Ted but it's a case of each to his own. Mitch is a fairly fit sort of bloke.

After playing the England test and injuring my shoulder, I stayed on only for the test in France before coming home but looking on I didn't really get a feeling of what Mitch and Deans were trying to achieve, say with the World Cup in mind.

I think it was a little too early to figure out what was taking shape then but by 2003 that became more evident. They tried a lot of players so that gave them a

Cully wasn't well treated by John Mitchell and Robbie Deans. For some reason they seemed to have something against him.

decent idea of the talent that was available. From that 2002 touring team only a few ultimately survived but I still thought the exercise was worthwhile.

I think Cully was hard done by on that tour. He ended up starting only the test in France but he was easily the most experienced fullback in the side and I certainly believed he still had plenty to offer – if he'd been given the chance. It would have been good to have him there in the test against England although Mitch and Robbie probably looked at Ben Blair for his goalkicking as well for that match.

I couldn't say Cully was deliberately badly treated on that tour, or that he was left on the outer. What it came down to was probably far simpler than that. I just don't think Mitch and Robbie liked Cully at all. For some reason they had something against him. I don't know what that was but it was there. While they didn't like his style or something I had every belief that he was good for another year and, if looked after the right way, could have given the All Blacks value at the World Cup. Definitely.

There was also the sad story of the big guy. Jonah played really well in the England test but didn't figure so much from then on. Despite his health problems he never wanted any of us to treat him as a special case, he just wanted to be one of us.

I was lucky enough to be in quite a few All Black and Blues sides with him and he was a damned good team man. Outside team events, he was happy doing a lot of things on his own. He prepared in a different way to a lot of people. My preparation wasn't necessarily the same as the average player either but he was a great guy to talk to and of all the players I'd been involved with him as long as anyone, probably longer. Remember, we'd been together in the 1992 New Zealand Secondary Schools side. The only other player still around in the All Black frame from that side was Carl Hoeft.

It was just a tragedy about his health with someone of that talent and at his age. He had a few more good years left in him. It was sad it had to finish that way for Jonah in an All Black jersey on that tour. Everything was at a low for him and wasn't going right. It was a real shame. I'm sure he would have wanted to finish in better style and I felt sorry for him. He'd given so much to the All Black jersey and he deserved a better farewell. He'd also done unbelievable things for the Blues in the earlier days as well.

Jonah was under incredible pressure in England with all the attention he faced there. Everyone wanted a piece of him. He handled it well, though. The value placed on him over there was fairly unbelievable to see. They worship him over there. There's no question he was the biggest name I have been involved with in my career.

When he was at his peak with the Blues Jonah was so awesome. We gave him a lot of ball then but it was a lot harder to use him as well as that in test matches. There's so much more pressure on you and the style of game is different.

Jonah came right back into things in the 2002 test against England. Despite his health problems he never wanted us to treat him any differently.

Maybe sometimes he was used too much as a battering ram. It was a fairly understandable tactic to try to attract extra players in to tackle him, look for quick ball. It was probably a matter of finding a balance in how to use him. In what became his third to last test – the one against England – we saw signs again of how good he could be when he was used as an attacking weapon.

While Cully and Jonah had moved out of the picture I knew I still had a chance even though my tour was cut short by my shoulder injury. I'd found out the obvious way I had a place in the plans through the basic action of being selected and it went from there. I had no forewarning of what Mitch was up to, no phone call or chat somewhere along the way to let me know.

I'd gathered from the Twickenham test that I was in their thinking but, because I was injured straightaway and didn't do the whole tour, I couldn't be sure. Over the years, Mehrts and I have often been in the picture together at first five while Tony Brown also figured at one stage. The situation's not a lot unlike what went on with Foxy and Frano Botica in the 1980s and early '90s. There was only room for one of them and that basically ended up being Foxy. So much so that Frano decided to head off to play rugby league for Wigan.

I suppose there are differences in the way Mehrts and I play the game but even though he has been there all the time I never felt I was on the outer when it came to All Black selection. If I had thought that I probably would have got out of New Zealand rugby long ago. I was always inspired and determined to get back into the All Blacks.

I wasn't involved at all in the home tests in 2002 or the Tri Nations Cup so I wasn't sure where I fitted then but I still had belief I could get back in. That chance came when the door was opened for me making the end of year tour. The biggest priority after that was to make the 2003 Rugby World Cup squad but to do that I had to play well in the 2003 Super 12.

With a more settled structure the Blues certainly came back at last in 2003. Peter Sloane was still coach and Fitzy was manager again with Bruce Robertson brought in as assistant and Ted was there in the same job he'd done for Auckland in the NPC. After four ugly years, the elements fell into place with just one loss – to the Highlanders – before we dealt to the Brumbies 42-21 in our semi-final and stuck at it to beat the Crusaders 21-17 in a really tense final.

While Mitch wasn't giving me any signs privately, he was making media comments that I was definitely being looked at as first five material in the test side and at the same time Mehrts obviously wasn't seeing much time on the field with the Crusaders. Of course, I noticed what was going on there and soon enough I was picked at first five for the tests we had against England, Wales and France. That was a good way for me to start, having that chance, in World Cup year to get my foot in the door in what became the busiest All Black year of my career.

Mitch had a big thing about the journey we were on but I was more interested in his coaching than the way he spoke.

CHAPTER 11

The Journey Starts Here

JOHN MITCHELL AND HIS JOURNEY – everyone heard all about that in 2003. I know it's a word that attracted a lot of comment and criticism but it never bothered me when he used the term, or any of the other words he came up with. Each to his own and he had his way of talking which wasn't an issue the way I saw it. "The journey" became part of our operation and one we all lived with.

Mitch's journey, and our journey, had three well-publicised tours on the way – the three tests in June against England, Wales and France kicked it off followed by the Tri Nations Cup and then the Rugby World Cup.

Journey is a term I could easily use for my entire rugby career, and especially the All Black part of it which hasn't always had as many high spots as I'd like. It had certainly been erratic until 2003. Considering I made my All Black debut as long ago as 1995, the numbers emphasised how irregularly I was able to gain selection. In the eight seasons up to 2003, I'd managed just 24 total appearances in the jersey of which only 15 were tests.

It said something about a lot of things that in 2003 I would finish up almost doubling my number of test appearances to 29. First that said so much about the nature of the year it was with the Rugby World Cup the climax – a year in which we were to play 14 tests. It also said something for me personally that I was able to play in every one of the games, and I was honoured to do so. In the simplest form there was potential for 14 test victories the way we approached it. No matter where or when, we aim to win every test we play. That never changes even when there's a greater goal we're striving for, like the Webb Ellis Cup.

But in doing the groundwork to reach that point, I wasn't too clear at first about how we were aiming to achieve the goal or what the expectations were of me. There was, in fact, very little direct communication at any stage, either before I came back into the All Black team at the end of 2002 or in 2003 when it became evident I had a definite role to play. There weren't too many signposts on this journey the way I saw it. All I knew was that I was in the team.

If anything the lead-up to the first phase was a bit strained and I didn't feel we were ever that well-prepared for the tests against England, Wales and France – definitely not for the first of them at Wellington's Westpac Stadium. Because everything followed on so soon after the Super 12, it seemed a bit rushed to me and I had a concern we weren't that well-set for it. It couldn't be helped I guess but for those of us involved in the Super 12 final – and there were lots of us from the Blues and the Crusaders – there wasn't that much time to move from one demanding mission to another.

A camp we had at Mount Maunganui was valuable for helping to bring us together a bit. It wasn't purely training. There were also some bonding activities like kayaking and we also did some paddling in outrigger canoes. The trainers are always looking out for ways to keep us interested. Sometimes players will come up with a suggestion but the trick is to find things most of the group will enjoy. We tried a different outing with the Blues when we were in Sydney for a pre-season match before the 2004 Super 12 – we played lawn bowls. That was real fun, huge humour. The challenge with any activity, though, is to ensure most of the guys will get into it. There's nothing worse than having half a dozen guys moaning and saying: "What are we doing this for?"

In truth, activities were the last thing we really needed to think about. In a year

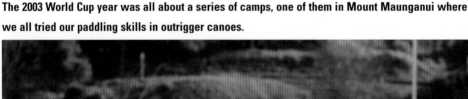

The 2003 World Cup year was all about a series of camps, one of them in Mount Maunganui where we all tried our paddling skills in outrigger canoes.

when the World Cup means so much there's nothing quite as demanding as facing one of the real favourites, straight up and cold as such. It grabs your attention when you know you're going to face a team with Martin Johnson, Lawrence Dallaglio, Jonny Wilkinson, Jason Robinson and the rest of the crew in those white jerseys.

As a one-off test with no warm-up match for us, this was going to ask some questions of us. One of the challenges in rugby's modern era is the huge number of one-off tests that are on the calendar and aren't part of a tournament. You want to win them. There's nothing like winning and winning builds confidence. But I can understand why a lot of people, especially those with more of a history in the game, miss seeing the All Blacks play a series.

A real effort is made to fit in quite a few countries on the international calendar in any one year. If you look back over recent seasons, more often than not three countries are brought out for one-off tests and, if test series are to become regular events again, then fewer nations would be in circulation. I guess that's what has to be balanced up.

Still, it's an attraction for everyone – not least the players – that the Lions will be touring for three tests and other matches in 2005. It's a long way off for me to be thinking about but, if I'm given the chance, that campaign would definitely have appeal. I'd also like to think the All Blacks will be far better-prepared for that event than we were for the test against England in 2003.

They came here as a match-hardened unit, a genuine combination and a winning one after beating the big three Southern Hemisphere teams at Twickenham in late 2002 before going on to win the Six Nations Championship again.

In many respects, we were chucked together for a match of this standard. We had a lot of players in the side who hadn't played together before and, in a few cases, hadn't played a test at all. Ma'a Nonu came in for his test debut at centre, so did Joe Rokocoko on the wing while Mils Muliaina was set to have his first test off the bench. Doug Howlett was pushed to fullback, Tana Umaga to second five and Rodney So'oialo and Ali Williams were still fairly new to test rugby as well, with minimal exposure on the Northern Hemisphere tour in late 2002. The other six guys around them in the pack had all missed that tour – Richie McCaw, Reuben Thorne, Chris Jack, Greg Somerville, Anton Oliver and Dave Hewett – so there wasn't a real combination there.

With time tight, we were also struggling to get a game plan together that we could use for the rest of the year so it was difficult in that first match trying to put something in place that everyone felt comfortable with. We'd all come together from different teams in the Super 12 and suddenly we had to work as a unit for the first test of the year against England, of all teams.

On the night we stuck in there and it was only through my poor goalkicking

Above: England flanker Richard Hill lines me up in the 2003 test in Wellington. We were beaten 15-13 on a night when I simply didn't kick well enough.

Right: Of all the players the All Blacks have used at halfback, Justin Marshall's easily the most experienced. He's been there in most of the tests I've played.

that we lost the match 13-15. Jonny Wilkinson kicked well that night, really well, especially for people who like their rugby like that – four penalties and a dropped goal. Beautiful, some would say. The wind was challenging but he handled it almost perfectly while I didn't hit the ball well at all. The suggestion was made that I was being affected by a shoulder problem. That wasn't the reason. I just had one of those nights when I didn't kick well enough. Simple as that.

I guess it was fair to wonder why we didn't go for goal when we were awarded penalties in the second half with England down to 13 men for a stage after Neil Back and Dallaglio had been sent to the sin bin. At the time the score was 9-6 to England and there might have been an argument to have a shot. I didn't have a problem at all that we didn't. I thought it was great that the call was made to go for the scrum option. They were two men short. Why not? It was credit to England for keeping us out but we had to have a go for a five-pointer. You have to attack them in a situation like that. So it didn't work… well sometimes that's the way it goes but at least we gave it a go. I thought it was a good decision.

Some people believe that's not the way you play test match rugby. They say you need to have a test-match mentality about things, that you shouldn't take risks and must always play the percentages. That's what I don't understand. It's still the same game. It's rugby. The game doesn't change. You're on the same shaped field and you're out there for 80 minutes. I have a real problem with people tensing up in tests and not wanting to try things. It shouldn't be like that. I know a lot more hangs on the result but I don't see the point in shutting down like that. All that stuff worrying about the crowd and everything. I see it all the time with players in tests. I happen to have a different attitude. I say: "Give me the ball. I want to try something." That's how you play rugby. You try to do something when you have the ball. I don't think it's a case of other guys being nervous it's just that they keep talking about playing the test match way.

I try to say to the guys: "Let's do this, or let's do that." At the end of the day it's up to the captain, though. In that regard, Rushie (Xavier Rush) has been good with the Blues, especially in 2003. He offers me the chance to take a lot of shots at goal and I tend to say: "No, let's kick for the corner and go for the lineout." When you know you've got a team on the run, or when you're not in the game, you've got to get into it somehow and taking a penalty shot isn't going to do that for you very often. I'd rather take a lineout five metres out than go for a penalty if we're trying to get back into the contest. Let's have a go. And obviously if you're on top then you must go for the try. What use is a penalty then?

You should be able to gather I'm not a fan of penalties. Correct – and I don't like penalty-ridden games either. I reckon the value of the penalty should be dropped to one point or maybe two and make the dropped goal one. I can't understand how you can be given three points for a dropped goal. It's a soft option. It should be an option only to give you the chance to win a game when it's all locked up, or maybe to take a lead out to more than a converted try, say to eight points or maybe 15 points so your opponents need to score twice to get ahead again. That's my opinion on it. Lots of people are probably happy with the way it is but I'd love to see it changed because it would make the game more entertaining.

I'll cover myself a bit, though. Of course, I accept there are times when it's smart to have a penalty shot. If you've been under the hammer a bit it's a good chance for the players to gather themselves and have a rest. There is a time and place for penalties but I think we see far too many of them. You know when you're out there when the right time arises to go for goal; I just wish more players – or coaches and captains – decided that should be now and then rather than every time, or close to it.

So when we had England on deep defence and playing two men short at Westpac Stadium that night, the time wasn't right for a penalty. We could sense that we had to have a crack at them.

Our plan in that match had been to play a high-paced game, trying to move the big England forwards around as much as we could but there'd been a bit of rain and there was wind as well. That didn't help us in the way we wanted to go about it although we didn't do that badly actually. They weren't able to score a try against us. We were really close to beating them and we probably would have if I'd kicked a lot better. Most of all, if we'd had the time to be better-prepared we would have been right I'm sure.

As a step towards the World Cup, there was some merit in the effort but it was still a loss and we found ourselves under a lot of stress during the game. We never expected that kind of heat from Wales a week later in Hamilton and it proved to be nothing like the contest we had in Wellington.

I'd lost the goalkicking job to Daniel Carter but it didn't worry me in the slightest. If the coaching staff wanted someone else to kick, that was fine. I was just happy to be out there involved in the side. Just because I'd had a poor night in Wellington and wasn't wanted as the kicker the next game isn't something that would ever get me down, nor does it affect my confidence as a kicker. That's just a small thing. If I'm asked during a game to have a shot, sure, I'm happy to have a go, but it never worries me who is doing the kicking. Things just don't faze me the way they might other people.

We went a lot better against Wales, started to feel comfortable playing together and got a few things going in winning 55-3. From being uncertain before playing in Wellington, I could sense after the Hamilton match that we were developing something with the World Cup in mind. I thought the game plan was good and we improved a lot, although it had to be said we were facing a side that was-

Top: Daniel Carter provided us with another goalkicking option in World Cup year.

Above: Wales provided two different faces to us in 2003. In Hamilton, they posed no threat but at the World Cup it was to be another story.

n't anywhere near as demanding as England.

What we worked on within our game plan were the various themes we had – if one wasn't going well then we'd change to another one. We had a wide theme, a midfield theme or a close one involving the forwards. Either the halfback or I would call which one we would go for if we could see we needed to change something in the course of a match. They were the options we worked on from the start of our international campaign as we tried to finesse our game plan for the World Cup itself.

While themes were important, so was the leadership triangle Mitch and Robbie Deans put a lot of faith in it – Reuben (Thorne), Tana (Umaga) and Justin (Marshall). I was also called on to be a leader because of my playing role so we had plenty of guys to influence decisions or make decisions. The leaders would talk when they needed to, or they did until the Rugby World Cup semi-final. Tana's such a significant force not just for his leadership but his experience as well. In the Blues we had a rock like him in Eroni Clarke and you need a player like that. Tana doesn't say a lot. He leads with his actions. One of those actions showed the other side to him as person in Hamilton when he stopped to put Welsh captain Colin Charvis in the recovery position after he'd been knocked out in a Jerry Collins tackle. I didn't even see what he did at the time but it's another measure of the man.

If we thought we'd done a lot of useful things in Hamilton and had made some progress, we took a couple of steps back despite beating France 31-23 in Christchurch. Our set pieces weren't too good at all and you'll always struggle if that part of your game isn't up to standard. The lineout was a real issue for sure that night.

I think that test exposed one area where we couldn't match up as well as we'd like. When you looked at our forward pack, there wasn't a lot of bulk. We didn't and still don't have a big pack, especially in the lock department. It's a problem in New Zealand rugby that we don't have a lot to choose from in the way of genuinely big forwards. Brad Thorn has bulk but he's one of the real exceptions.

Our loose forward combination also came in for some criticism throughout the year but I thought there wasn't too much wrong with it at this stage. I have to say I wouldn't have minded seeing Brad given a shot at blindside flanker at some point, just to see what he was capable of there as another option. He could have been quite good there and it would have given us another ball runner. If we had a shortage in the way of forwards who had some bulk about them, then we also lacked a bit of aggression and mongrel in our forwards, especially the starting pack. We didn't have enough strong running guys to take the ball up. Kees Meeuws could do it but he was generally on the bench and obviously Brad was another but he was a bench player as well. In the starting pack we probably had only Jerry and Keven

Left: Big Brad Thorn gave us some real bulk but I wouldn't have minded seeing him tried as a blind-side flanker rather than being used at lock.

Below: There's no doubt Richie McCaw was way out in front as an open-side flanker throughout 2003. He's just an outstanding player.

Mealamu who had those qualities, which left us a bit short in that department.

The French showed us up in some of those aspects but, while it wasn't a sharp effort, we won, though, and there's never anything easy about the French no matter where or when you play them. Viewed overall, we started to develop some confidence out of those three games and I could see we had a game plan that could work as long as we got our set pieces right. That was the main thing.

In those three matches we were just building towards the Tri Nations and the World Cup, trying to put a game plan in place. The aim was to have everyone thinking down the same track and to build confidence within the team. They were still tests we were striving to win but in the overall plan they didn't matter too much.

That left us in reasonable shape for the Tri Nations Cup – a lot better than reasonable, as it turned out, because we got off to a banger in South Africa.

This was a test outcome where preparation was everything. That started with us spending a whole week in Durban before going to Pretoria. It's normal practice for us these days to be based in Durban for tests at altitude. It works far better for us that way and then we travel to Johannesburg or Pretoria just a couple of days before. Durban's a nice place to stop off as well. We were in a nice hotel with the beach right there so the guys could just chill out a bit there and it definitely

Our 2003 Tri Nations Cup campaign couldn't have started any better when we ripped South Africa apart in Pretoria. I was among the try-scorers in an incredible display.

gives us the right preparation.

When it came to game time at Loftus Versfeld, everything seemed to fly and work out to plan. We were on fire as the score-line of 52-16 would indicate. Other than the even preparation we had in Durban, I can't really say why we were so hot that day. It was just one of those games you have every now and then. This was also one of those games when the concerns we sometimes have about the size of our forwards simply didn't become an issue. Because we were able to dictate the flow and pace of the game, this never became a slug-out between the two packs. It didn't have time for that sort of confrontation with us keeping the game so fluid.

It was still a concern, though, and we suspected it would prove to be more of an issue at some point during the year. For whatever reason we just can't match it physiologically with say England, France, South Africa or the Wallabies at times. They seem to have such big forwards and over the course of almost any season that has cost us, and hurt us.

When it comes to the crunch and a forward pack gets out there and just gives it to you, especially a bigger pack than yours, you're going to come second. I think we've struggled the last few years. The last time I can remember an All Black forward pack being feared would have been in 1997 and I don't think that's been the case ever since. That's what we're lacking. Okay, we get away with it and win some games but in the crunch games when teams want it more than us, we're probably going to lose all the time.

Whatever you might have in the backline, you need a degree of ascendancy in the forwards. You can't just rely on individual brilliance. It doesn't come or work that way all the time. It would be good to have more size and strength in the forwards to provide some dominance but we really haven't had that for the last five or six years. We've had brilliant players, individuals, in the forwards but we haven't had an eight that's been solid together and feared.

From everything I've ever heard, it's nothing like what it was in the 1960s or in parts of the 1970s. And I know we're well short of what the All Black pack was like in the late '80s and especially in the '90s when we had names like the Brookes, Brown, Dowd, Fitzpatrick, Kronfeld and Michael and Ian Jones. Opponents used to fear that pack and through it we could be assured of something like 65 per cent of possession. We haven't seen it like that for too long. In the really big games it's a battle to gain parity in possession. We might have to function on 45 per cent of the ball. It might be a little more every now and then. It just depends on how each match pans out.

I suppose the way our forward play has gone can often be measured by what's seen in the Super 12 at times. Teams like the Crusaders for quite a few years and the Blues in 2003 could put it together up front but then you look at what hap-

Dougy (Howlett) had plenty to like about a rare day-time test in Pretoria. We won 52-16 and he scored two of our seven tries.

pened with the Blues at the start of the 2004 Super 12. Our forwards were turning over so much ball. We're just not as consistently accurate and effective as we used to be. Not just in test football but at Super 12 level, New Zealand teams aren't as efficient in their set piece work either.

In many ways people saw the 2004 Super 12 as New Zealand's chance to start all over again after what happened in the Rugby World Cup but it certainly didn't work out that way early on.

There are exceptions, as I say. There are times when our forwards have really aimed up and taken care of forward packs that might have more size but not the same mobility. The 2003 Tri Nations test in Pretoria was one of them when our guys just blew them right away. I think we moved them around and, when you have a forward pack, a big one like the South Africans one, we like to keep it fluid and to go wide. Maybe their big guys struggled with that. It's all very well being big and strong but you have to be able to get around the field as well. They couldn't handle it and with that kind of advantage it was a fairly easy win, the backs scoring six of the seven tries.

Then we had the same outcome just a week later against the Wallabies at Telstra Stadium in Sydney, a venue that hasn't been all that kind to us in recent history. This match didn't start well either with Australia scoring first but from then on it was basically a replica of what happened in Pretoria, this time the backs scoring all

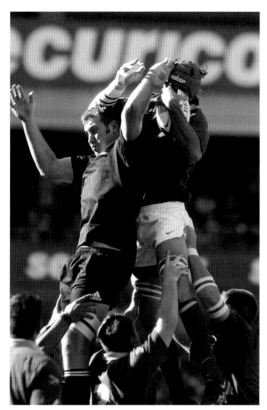

A rare sight in our first Tri Nations test in 2003 as South Africa secures some lineout possession.

seven tries in a 50-21 win.

We'd gone into the Tri Nations wanting to win it. There was a trophy we wanted and that was the first one we were after. The theory was bandied around later that the Wallabies didn't have a total focus on the Tri Nations, that they were looking further ahead to the World Cup. I don't know about that. I know we weren't. What they were doing didn't really bother us at all. For us it was first things first and we wanted to win the Tri Nations, simple as that. After that we'd look at our next goal. Whether the Australians were or not, I don't know.

What I do know is that we'd exceeded our expectations in the first two away matches. Not by winning them. We expected nothing less than victory in both games. It was more to do with the manner of our displays. We'd muddled through a lot of the time in the tests in June but then suddenly we seemed to explode once we were away from home. Maybe it was just that – being away from home with fewer pressures around you all the time and having the chance to zone in on what we're doing.

This was a strange campaign, though. From being freewheeling in the away games, the return matches in Dunedin and Auckland couldn't have been more contrasting. That could have had something to do with playing at night under lights in the first instance at Carisbrook and rain was a factor in Auckland. Yet in both cases, the South Africans and the Wallabies were right into us in a way they hadn't been on their home grounds, not that we gave them much of a chance then.

First it was the Springboks in Dunedin and this was one of those times when they were possessed. Along with the French, the South Africans have a rare ability to hit another level in passion and intensity when they're in the mood. They were certainly in that frame of mind that night. They're so tough when they're like that. They got stuck right into us from the opening seconds and pressured us in every part of the game.

As if that wasn't enough, there was South African prop Richard Bands, a bloke

I won't forget for a long time. I'm still seeing him now. He must have steamed 40 metres for his try with someone with No 10 on his back one of those who tried unsuccessfully to stop him. He just ran right over me.

It was one of those nights when you had to grind it out for the full 80 minutes, nothing like Pretoria or Sydney in the weeks before it. You get those. They're all part of rugby. This one had just one try apiece – Joe Rokocoko with ours – while I was able to kick every goal in a 19-11 win, and this was a game when the penalties did matter. That night in Wellington suddenly seemed like it happened a long time ago. What it also meant was that the Tri Nations Cup was ours again.

We were happy to get the win that night. I know South African rugby hasn't been in great shape in the time I've been playing but I think that has more to do with their administration than anything. They've got the players. They just aren't running the game so well there. Every time you play them in a test, they're still as aggressive as ever.

That set up our next goal to regain the Bledisloe Cup. There's nothing wrong at all with having New Zealand's name on the Tri Nations Cup. It means a lot to us. Still, any All Black will tell you the Bledisloe Cup is at another level again.

I'm not sure the system is right at the moment where the holder just has to win one of the two Tri Nations matches each year to hold onto the cup. Put another way, the challenger has to win both games or at worst win one and draw one to claim the prize. That had been working in the Wallabies' favour for too long. They took it off us in 1998 and had held it ever since but there'd been occasions when the outcome had finished 1-1 across the two games. It always worked better when it was a three-test series. Then again, there's the challenge of squeezing an extra match into the calendar.

This time, though, we knew we had a decent shot at it. We'd won the first clash in Sydney and now history was also an extra element for the return match at Eden Park.

This encounter marked 100 years almost to the day that New Zealand had played and won its first rugby test on August 15, 1903 by beating Australia. So, quite a lot of fuss was made about the occasion with all sorts of functions held involving a huge number of former All Blacks and Wallabies. I know about it only because I've since been told about it but at the time I wasn't aware anything special was happening, to be honest. It didn't interest me because our minds were set on something we regarded as far more important, beating Australia to regain the Bledisloe Cup.

As a contest the game wasn't a lot unlike the battle with the Springboks in Dunedin a week earlier. This time we managed two tries, both to Doug Howlett, to Australia's solitary effort but it was another wrestle, not helped by rain. We looked to be comfortable at 21-9 but the Aussies had a sniff late when they pulled

Top: Keven Mealamu leaves George Gregan behind as he busts Australia's defence open on the night we reclaimed the Bledisloe Cup at Eden Park.
Above: Tana Umaga imposes himself with Doug Howlett looming up outside him. Dougy scored both of our tries in the 21-17 win over the Wallabies.

Opposite and above: It's fairly obvious what's happened here. At last our friend the Bledisloe Cup is where it should be after beating Australia 21-17 at Eden Park. After losing it in 1998, we'd waited for this but we still wanted an even bigger prize.

back to 21-17 before we held on for victory. I'm sure they wanted the win as much as we did, looking for some confidence before hosting the World Cup, but it was another one of those grinders and we always knew it was going to be like that. We knew it wouldn't be like the Sydney game again.

I've been involved in a lot of wins that mattered to teams I've played for; this was one of the best and one of the most significant. Of course, there was an even bigger prize we really wanted but this one was just fine on the night of August 16, 2003. The Bledisloe is obviously a great trophy to win because there's so much history involved in it but for me personally I would still say winning the test was actually more important than winning the prize. The trophy is a bonus while winning the game is everything.

Not that I wasn't thrilled about what we achieved that night. Of course I was and so was everyone else from the other players, coaching staff and management through to the New Zealand rugby public. We had an old friend back where we believed it belonged. The boys certainly chilled out, relaxed and enjoyed the occasion, celebrated the success.

Two goals, two achieved on this journey. We'd opened with six wins from seven tests played. No one could say the year hadn't started well. It was just about everything we wanted with just one loss so far. There were two outstanding performances in Pretoria and Sydney, two slugfests in Dunedin and Auckland, a cruise in Hamilton, a fairly scratchy effort in Christchurch and just the one that didn't go the way we planned in Wellington.

With seven tests played over almost three months, it was possible to get more of a handle on the coaching operation as well. I'd still have to say communication wasn't a strong point. I don't remember a time when there was any special effort put into sitting down to talk things through with me in a one-on-one way, no detailed discussion about what it was Mitch and Deans were looking for from me. I don't know that I needed it but it still never happened.

The one thing I knew now was that I wasn't seen as a fullback, not that I was told that directly. I just had to take that as read from the way the team was named for each test. Seven tests had been played and I'd had the No 10 jersey on in each of them. So, in that regard, I knew where I fitted in even though no one was talking to me about it.

I found Mitch a fairly quiet coach now that I'd been able to study his methods. I wouldn't have classed him as that much of a motivator. Graham Henry and John Hart were into motivation in an obvious way where Mitchell probably went for the calm approach. With him, it seemed we were expected to motivate ourselves but I must say I like to hear a motivational coach now and then. It depends what they have to say. Sometimes it's a player rather than the coach who can come up with the right message. You can be mucking around at training and one of the players might say something that means a lot. You grab hold of it and take it with you right through the week and into the game. Mitch wasn't so much of a contributor in that style. It was actually Deans who had more to say out on the training field in terms of organising and stuff.

Through working together with them for the past few months, we had a fair idea of who the 30 players would be when the World Cup squad was named. And, based on what had been going on up till then, there certainly wasn't anything too surprising when the final names were revealed.

But there were still a couple of players I felt for, guys I'd played a lot of rugby with from New Zealand Secondary Schools and New Zealand Colts days in the early 1990s. I'm talking about Anton Oliver and Christian Cullen. Since starting out, we'd gone on to see a lot together playing for the All Blacks as well and now they definitely wouldn't be going to the 2003 World Cup.

The decision to drop Anton for the Tri Nations was harsh I thought, especially on the basis of the one game against France in Christchurch. That was the coach's decision and I don't sit around and worry about those things but I felt

Coaches in arms Mitch and Robbie . . . they were never far apart and, after winning the Tri Nations and the Bledisloe Cup, they seemed to be on the right track.

sorry for him, especially with the experience he had and could have offered us in Australia in October–November. It wasn't to be and all you can do is to try to move on when things like that happen.

Mitchell made some fairly strong public comments about issues he had with the way both Anton and Christian had been playing. That was a tough way to go out for those players.

I've been in the situation when I haven't made teams but I think when that happens a phone call from the coach is always nice to let you know you haven't been selected but also to tell you why you haven't been, especially when you think you might have had at least a slight chance of being picked. It's just a courtesy thing.

Team announcements are always an issue I guess. Some coaches like to let all players know they've been chosen, or left out, before a side is announced publicly. Other coaches go the other way and don't tell anyone so they all find out when the team is announced live on television or radio. I don't mind the idea of making it a surprise for players that way. I think it's quite exciting having team announcements. I don't have a problem with it. But if a coach isn't going to choose someone, then I think he should let him know beforehand and again provide a reason.

What did happen with the naming of the World Cup squad was the confirmation that four really experienced All Blacks weren't going, although there had been indications for a long time before that they would miss out. You could make that five counting the big guy Jonah Lomu with the problems he had with his health. Apart from Anton and Cully, the other two were obviously Taine Randell and Andrew Mehrtens, again players who I'd had playing experiences with going back quite a few years now.

Could they have done a job for the All Blacks at the World Cup? Could the team have used their experience? We'll never know and it's not worth speculating about really. It's a hard game playing rugby at this level and picking teams to play. Someone has to miss out. Not everyone can get in. At the end of the day, it's up to the coaches and we have to respect that. Other people might have other views about who should be included but it doesn't matter in the end.

So many people have wondered ever since why Mehrts wasn't there. Would it have helped if he was? Look, I don't know. He certainly would have been a goal-kicking option although, then again, we had Daniel Carter there as well for that and to be honest it wasn't goalkicking that cost us in the end. Mehrtens' experience would have been useful in much the same way as Tana and he's a lively sort of bloke to have around as well as being a really good team man. Off the field he's an amusing guy who likes to have heaps of fun.

Whatever the arguments about their exclusion – and that was sad – we were still confident with the side we had and we'd proven there was also reason to be confident with our earlier performances. I think we certainly had the team. I know there's an argument about the experience we lost through not having Cully, Mehrts, Taine and Anton. Yes, they could count 216 tests between them and Jonah's problems robbed the side of another 63 tests but I didn't believe experience – or a lack of it – would be a factor in how we performed at the World Cup. What mattered most would be our ability and our commitment to adhere to the game plan we worked to put into place.

Before we were anywhere near that point we had a lot of territory to cover, literally. One of the major parts of our build-up programme was a series of camps around New Zealand before we headed to Australia. We had scheduled stops in Whangarei, Auckland, Gisborne, New Plymouth, Nelson and then Terrace Downs near Methven.

The Gisborne visit was a wash-out. We never went there at all after a deluge swamped the place. That was a real shame for both the locals and for us because the whole operation was really good value, although I can't say I enjoyed the Methven stop. We were stuck in the middle of nowhere there with nothing to do. You'd finish your training and just go back to your room. That was it. That was the most boring aspect of the whole programme going there. It might have been fine if you wanted to play golf every day but it snowed, it was cold and windy and it rained as well. That part of it wasn't well thought out.

I liked going to the provincial cities, though. There were things to do there.

Should Mehrts have made the World Cup squad? I don't know. He would have been a goalkicking option but I don't think it was goalkicking that cost us in the end.

You could walk down the street, we had a public training session at each location and you got a sense from the locals that they were happy to see us in their town and they also seemed to be confident about the World Cup. We had sufficient reasons to be confident we had a decent shot at it as well. So far, we'd done all we could to stay on course on the journey to win the World Cup – now there was just one destination left.

If there was one sight we didn't need in our very first match of the World Cup it was this image of Tana Umaga. He didn't play again after injuring his knee against Italy.

CHAPTER 12

What World Cup?

A T HOME, THE ALL BLACKS' World Cup caravan kept moving from place to place. In Australia, it arrived in one place and never moved – Melbourne. Nice city actually. I didn't mind it. Good for shopping I'd say, not that I did much of that, well not for the people who wish I had anyway (apparently I stand accused of finding time to buy only a suit for myself). It was all Aussie Rules there and not a lot of people had any idea about what was going on with the Rugby World Cup, or even what it was for that matter. You could walk around and no one knew who you were or why you were there. That side of it was good for us at the start of the tournament but I suppose after about four or five weeks it was time to move on – only we didn't, we stayed there.

That's where there was a problem. I thought the guys became a bit stale and ran out of things to do to keep them occupied. The way the schedule was mapped out, we were likely to be in Melbourne for the quarter-finals – which we were – but once that was over I think we should have moved out and gone to Sydney. That would become increasingly obvious to me the further the tournament went.

Initially, though, there was plenty to like about being in the Victorian capital. Our first two pool games against Italy and Canada were there before we made hit-and-run trips to Brisbane to play Tonga and to Sydney to face Wales. They were just flying visits before returning to Melbourne. Even after our quarter-final the plan for the rest of the tournament was to go back and forth to Sydney.

Our campaign didn't have a start that seemed too difficult with pool games against Italy, Canada, Tonga and Wales. They were all opponents we were expected to beat and beat well basically. Outsiders might wonder how we set ourselves for tests against opposition teams ranked lower than us. The truth is you prepare differently for every side but I can say it's not hard getting up for any game like that, especially when you're at the World Cup. They're all test matches and I love playing rugby any time. It's what I do and it's what I enjoy. It's always exciting for me.

So what of the pool games?

The first one against Italy wasn't memorable for the result – the win came easily enough – but for Tana Umaga's knee injury. I'd started the match back on goalkicking duties, only that didn't last long after I'd collided with Tana. The end result was a haematoma on my right hip and I struggled through the whole game but my problem was nothing compared to Tana's. In the heat of the moment, I didn't think too much about what had happened to him but afterwards, when we knew he might well be out for the rest of the tournament, it was gut-wrenching. It was a killer blow for him when you knew he had been building up to this for the whole year and then that happened in the very first game at the World Cup. It was so much like what I'd experienced at the 1999 World Cup so I knew how he felt. My tournament was over completely then. In the end, Tana's was, too, although he did stay on with us.

He was so important to us and from that moment on we missed him. Big-time. When you play with Tana he gives you so much – his voice, his experience and, as a midfielder, he's solid. He's a game-breaker and he lifts guys around him. He always talks to me a lot; he talks to everyone. His experience makes him such a good communicator, talking it up big on both attack and defence. Tana's such a strong player defensively, a big unit who really provides strength for us when he's playing. He leads by his actions.

Of course, we felt sorry for Tana but we couldn't dwell on it. We had to move forward from what had happened to him. At the same time, there was also some hope that he might come back later in the tournament so he stayed on for treatment. It was valuable keeping him on because he was able to pass on advice and help in a number of ways. If it was getting him down, he hid it well. He obviously didn't want to bring the team down with him I guess although I'm sure deep down he was hurting; the guys were hurting for him as well but he kept things moving along.

Initially Ma'a Nonu looked a strong prospect as Tana's replacement, going really well when he came on against Italy and then playing against Tonga as well. After that he was never tried again. Despite being a dangerous runner, the coaching staff had other plans.

It was significant that our original World Cup squad included three fullback options in Mils Muliaina, Leon MacDonald and Ben Blair but, like me four years earlier, Ben was injured and out of the tournament without even playing a game. He was meant to be on the bench for the opening match against Italy only for a

I'm not one for remembering too much about games I've played. Our 2003 World Cup match against Canada was one of them.

scan to reveal he had a serious neck injury (a prolapsed disc), ending his involvement. Rather than bringing in another fullback to replace Ben, another centre – my Auckland team-mate Ben Atiga – was brought over giving us more midfield cover in Tana's absence.

If there were reasons to remember the Italy match, the next outing against Canada came and went without either incident or anything particularly memorable about the level of our performance. I'd have to say the same about the encounter with Tonga. They're just not games I remember all that well.

By the time I'd played those three games, I had appeared in each one of the 10 tests the All Blacks had played in the year. It wasn't an issue to me that I was playing all the time. I appreciate people suggested I could have been rested or left out every now and then had Andrew Mehrtens been part of the team. That actually had nothing to do with the fact I was being picked all the time. If the coaching staff had wanted they had other guys to put in at first-five instead of me like Daniel Carter and Aaron Mauger. It's nice to have a rest now and then but I certainly wasn't bothered playing every game. I enjoyed it.

Those first three matches worked out fairly well for us. We achieved most of what we wanted and I thought we were travelling well knocking up scores of 70-7 against Italy, 68-6 over Canada and 91-7 in the clash against Tonga.

That was all reasonably predictable but what happened in our last pool game in Sydney was totally unexpected, certainly from people outside the team. I don't think many at all considered the Welsh would give us such a hurry-up at Telstra Stadium.

We like to believe we prepare well for all opponents but I think we were also caught a bit unaware by Wales. Maybe we had become a little bit complacent for that match. Yes, we probably under-estimated them, but I'd always give them credit for the way they took the game to us; they played bloody well that night. In actual fact, I thought it was beneficial for us to have a match like that after our earlier pool games.

In those high-scoring encounters things became a bit loose at times, which wasn't surprising. The Welsh, though, gave us a wake-up. They really ran at us and played just the same way in their quarter-final against the Poms. You look at those two games and Wales took a huge step up.

It was fairly obvious the Welsh coach Steve Hansen had a really decent look at the way we'd played in the test in Hamilton earlier in the year and worked out exactly what was needed. At the same time, there were a reasonable number of changes in the Welsh line-up, one which wasn't what many regarded as their No 1 combination. If it was a little unbelievable for our supporters looking on at the ground or watching back home on television, we were a bit stunned as well. All the Welsh players excelled but I guess the winger Shane Williams and the New Zealand-born centre Sonny Parker were two who made the greatest impact.

Before the match, no one would have believed Wales would put so much heat on us and lead as they did early in the second half, but stranger things have happened – and this was for real.

Despite the way the Welsh were hitting us, I never thought we were in trouble to the point we could lose the match. It didn't feel like that out in the middle and gradually we worked our way back into the contest. We knew we just had to hang with them, minimise the damage, stick to a solid plan and the match would turn eventually, which it did as we went on to win 53-37 – but, boyo, it was still some test. It was one of those nights when it was difficult to stop them but that didn't matter so much as long as we kept scoring some points as well.

Four matches gone, four wins and we'd scored more than 280 points and conceded very few, other than against Wales. Did that mean we were vulnerable then for the quarter-finals? I wouldn't have thought so. The pool games had worked out according to plan apart from a tickle-up from the Welsh and I was sure that had been valuable for us rather than a cause for concern.

What it also meant was that the real business was next, the sudden-death phase of the tournament and yet another chance to tangle with the Springboks who were coming off a decent performance when they blew Manu Samoa away. It came at a cost, though, because they lost one of their best players, flanker Joe van Niekerk, not that we were so bothered about that.

All we knew was that we were in a situation where losing to South Africa now would be the end for us. We'd be on our way home. We talked all week about that. Beating them twice in the Tri Nations a few months earlier counted for zip now. We also talked all week about one other need – we had to step up from what had gone on before in the tournament. And on November 8 we did just that.

We played well that night, really well. Maybe we could have finished more off but 29-9 against South Africa? I'd take a 20-point margin over them every time. We made the South Africans look poor, making them play the way we wanted them to play. Our forwards asserted themselves giving us even more confidence. That was the best game we'd played in the whole tournament and to me a sign of good things to come. After that I believed we could go on with it.

What it brought about was another chapter in the most frequent match-up in our international history, another battle with our Australian neighbours. A few months earlier, we'd been at each other for the 118th time with the Bledisloe Cup on the line at Eden Park. Now we were set to go again on November 15, 2003, this time at Telstra Stadium in Sydney in a match that meant plenty to both of us.

We didn't lack strike power throughout 2003, especially from left winger Joe Rokocoko who kept crossing the line at will.

Jerry Collins belts it up in our quarter-final win over the Springboks, our best performance at the World Cup.

We wanted it and needed it to put the All Blacks into a World Cup final for the third time and give us a shot at regaining the prize a whole nation wanted. It didn't matter what had happened to the Wallabies earlier in the year in the Tri Nations or in this tournament. We still respected them and saw them as a threat. You couldn't get away from the fact it was basically their tournament, they were the defending champions and so they had so much to play for, too.

Just the same, we hadn't seen anything from the Wallabies to concern us. Like us, they'd had a couple of soft games putting 90 on Romania and 142 on Namibia. They'd been only so-so beating Argentina and had barely sneaked past Ireland 17–16 in their last pool game before dealing with Scotland in their quarter-final.

In the lead-up to the semi, there was some speculation about whether Tana might be involved. We didn't get the feeling he would because he never really trained with the combination named for the match. Maybe the management were thinking of saving him for the final if we made it. Only the coaches knew what they had in mind on that.

On the training field he looked to be running fine. I couldn't see too many problems and he told me he was ready to play – then again, I suppose anyone would do that. I know I'd be telling everyone I was fine to play, especially if it was a World Cup semi-final.

So would he have been worth a punt on for that match? Do you risk his injury even more or do you gamble on him being right for the final instead? I don't know. Do you take a risk with someone who's probably not right or go with someone who's 100 per cent? At the end of the day I was just glad that wasn't my decision. I don't know what I would have done if it was up to me. Instead it was a call the coaches and Doc (John Mayhew) had to make and they made one. I think it was a tough one to make.

Imagine if Tana had been used and been injured again then the crap would have been flying for playing him when he wasn't right. What if he'd lasted only five minutes? And the idea of maybe having him on the bench would have left a lot of questions as well. I'm sure the coaches asked themselves all those questions over and over before going the way they did. The public doesn't see that.

Having made that decision the starting line-up named was Mils Muliaina at fullback, Joe Rokocoko and Doug Howlett as the wingers, Leon MacDonald and Aaron Mauger in the midfield, me at first five, Justin Marshall at half-back, Jerry Collins on the back of the scrum, Reuben Thorne and Richie McCaw the flankers, Ali Williams and Chris Jack the locks and a front row of Greg Somerville, Keven Mealamu and Dave Hewett. Was it the best possible line-up we could put together at that stage of the tournament? I suppose it was the only one that had the best combination, one that had been together for the last three games. At that stage it would have been hard to bring either Ma'a or Mils into centre. Ma'a hadn't been used since the match against Tonga and, while Mils has played a lot of football at centre, he hadn't been used there at the World Cup so now probably wasn't

I'm glad it wasn't my call to decide whether Tana Umaga should have been used in our World Cup semi-final against the Wallabies.

the time to be considering him. There were plenty of possibilities, only the timing wasn't quite right I guess. At least that was probably the reasoning.

The forward pack looked fine. If there had been some concerns about our forwards and the size of the pack, it wasn't an issue against South Africa a week earlier. They'd taken care of them no trouble at all so there was no need to think about changing the starting line-up by bringing in, say, Brad Thorn or Kees Meeuws. You'd say the South Africans had a more physical pack than the Wallabies and, as a coach, you would have said we did well against a physical South African pack so I'm sure we'll do well against the Aussies. Why change a winning combination?

Something else that wasn't going to change at this stage of the campaign was our media strategy. Throughout the tournament there was evidently some grumbling about us not being readily available to the media and that our image wasn't all it could be. I actually thought we did enough in that regard. We had the media in once a week and training was open to them once a week as well. I didn't see anything wrong with it.

Still, it became an issue again in the lead-up to the semi-final, especially after some comments made by former Australian international Sam Scott-Young about how the Wallabies should target "that snooty little guy with the tattoos, niggle him, smash him in defence, mess up his hair and he'll get cranky". After those comments had been published I was asked to appear at a media conference but I knew what the reporters wanted to ask me and I just didn't want to get involved in it. That was the reason I didn't front. I told our media man Matt McIlraith that

Another media conference for John Mitchell and Robbie Deans . . . there was criticism of our media strategy in 2003 but I didn't see a lot wrong with it.

I'd rather not do it and just stay out of the media that week so I could prepare my own way and concentrate on the semifinal. That was all there was to it as far as I was concerned. I wasn't trying to be rude nor was I ducking for cover. I simply believed it wasn't worth me getting involved in it.

I actually never had too many concerns about the media throughout the year. There were plenty of critical comments made about the way we performed in some of the earlier tests at home – especially against England and France – but that's all part of it. I don't worry about that. There's some rough stuff said but you have to do your best to accept it. There's not much you can do about it. It's there one day and gone the next. Fish and chip paper. There's a fair bit of good stuff that's written and said among some of the material that's harder to take. Cop it on the chin, I say. To me, it's all part of sport. You might not like it sometimes but it's there and it's not going to go away. It's really only the people who aren't informed who irritate the most.

We didn't need comments from anyone outside the team to remind us this would be the most difficult match of all. We were probably the favourites, which probably wasn't a good thing either. If the team we had, and the way we'd performed left us in good shape, our training that week in Melbourne was also right on the mark before we headed to Sydney late in the piece. There was nothing then to suggest we weren't ready.

If I had a misgiving, though, it was the fact we were still in Melbourne when I really felt we should have spent the whole week of the semifinal in Sydney, where we could have got among it and really felt what the event was all about. I think it's great to be in the atmosphere of a big occasion like that. It lifts you and gets you excited. Instead we were in Melbourne where no one really cared and we were just doing our own thing.

Maybe it served to make us a little complacent where we would have been more on edge if we'd been in Sydney. It meant we were in Melbourne for something like five weeks going into the semi against the Wallabies. On non-match days, our routine usually consisted of one training run and then you could go into town and check out the shops, although there's only so much shopping a bloke can do. We did things like go-karting and we also had a day at Flemington on Melbourne Cup day but it's a bit dreary when most of your time is built around staying in the same place, training at the same ground and doing that for five weeks.

It was just too long in one place and too long in a city where there was no feeling the World Cup was on. I had always assumed before we left for the World Cup that if we made the semis we would be moving completely to Sydney but I think that might have changed during the tournament.

And the way events played out at Telstra Stadium, I'd say the Melbourne factor was a more significant contributor to our downfall than anyone might have imagined...

CHAPTER 13

Dream is Over - Again

SOMETHING WASN'T RIGHT. I could sense it. It didn't add up with the occasion but it was still there. Here we were looking at the biggest match of the year for us so far, for most of us the most important game of our careers – other than the Rugby World Cup final we wanted to be in – and yet we just didn't seem ready for it.

I could feel it the moment we arrived at Telstra Stadium that evening on November 15, 2003. New Zealanders in Sydney, back at home and in other parts of the world were all willing us to become world champions for the first time since 1987. Of course, there was nothing more we wanted either. For that to happen we first had to contend with the Wallabies – but something was missing.

I knew that for sure when we headed onto the field to do our warm-ups. Kiwi fans were everywhere, the stadium was filling up and there was noise all around. But there wasn't any noise from us. We were quiet. We weren't up for some reason and I couldn't pick why. When we went through our grids there was none of the yelling, encouragement and excitement, not the way there usually is. There wasn't any spark. It was just: "Yeah, pop, pop, here... yeah, pop here". There wasn't the sound of the guys being up for it, and there should have been.

But there was from the Aussies. When I went up to halfway to try a few kick-offs, they were going through their warm-ups nearby and the excitement in their camp was unbelievable. I knew then that we were in trouble.

I didn't feel affected personally. I was still on edge and ready for the game but

Reuben Thorne's expression is enough on its own. There was nothing more painful than our World Cup semi-final loss to the Wallabies in Sydney.

I knew as a team we weren't right. When we went back into the dressing room we were still quiet, even in the minutes just before walking out. The guys weren't building each other up. They were just keeping to themselves, doing their own thing. I tried to convince myself it might be a good sign, that maybe it was a case of them getting themselves ready in a calmer way.

Nothing changed when we walked out onto the field beside the Wallabies. They were fizzing. You didn't have to be a genius to realise that. We were cool and I didn't like it.

Same when the national anthems were sung. The Aussies were into it, we weren't.

Same the moment the match started. They were into, we weren't. If we'd been quiet as a team before the game, we started it just as quietly. The Wallabies got stuck into us, starting the way I'd heard them in their warm-ups – excited. I knew then, that early in the match, that they had us.

It's not that we were right out of the game from the outset. We went close to scoring tries on both flanks before Stirling Mortlock intercepted my pass and went 80-odd metres for his try. How did that affect me? Not a lot. It was early enough in the game that it didn't bother me for long. Of course it gutted me when it happened but you have to say to yourself: "Move on". That's what I always do. You have to. You can't afford to let it get to you.

While Mortlock's try put a bit of doubt on things we came back to score a try ourselves leaving us just 7-13 down at halftime. That was it, though. We didn't really fire any shots after that.

Apart from two early scoring chances and then when Reuben scored, we hadn't really done anything in the first half. It felt like we weren't in it. As for the second half, well it was just all penalties – three to them and one for us – with not a lot going on with us at all. We weren't talking enough either – quiet before the game and quiet during it. That had a lot to do with the flow of the game. Things weren't going right so we weren't as vocal as we would normally be.

I thought we'd done well to even stay close to them for so long because Mortlock was causing us strife, the two wingers Wendell Sailor and Lote Tuqiri were coming in and doing so much work, too, that we were always going backwards. They went for me down the inside channels bringing their wingers in and we knew they would. They always do that. They had all the go-forward and did us all over the park. We couldn't get anything going.

It's said a lot about sport that one side wants it more than the other. It was easy to figure out which team that was on November 15.

In all the post-mortems all we kept hearing was how critical people were of us for not having a Plan B in that game. That's stupid. Of course, we had options.

Our overall approach was based on a fast-paced game with lots of ball move-

The Wallabies had plenty of traffic running at us in our World Cup semi-final, not least Wendell Sailor.

ment but within our plan we had themes. If one wasn't working, we'd change theme. So in certain circumstances we could go to a wide theme, a midfield theme or a close one for the forwards. We'd always go to whatever was required, a call either Justin or I would make. So in the semi-final I tried to switch the play in close with inside balls, looking to bring the forwards back into the game but the Aussies just answered everything we came up with.

There were also leadership problems for us. When we were at full strength we had what Mitch called a leadership triangle revolving around Reuben as the captain, Justin at halfback and Tana in the midfield. They were three experienced players who all had a voice when they were on the field. Obviously Tana wasn't there against the Wallabies and Justin was injured during the match so that broke down.

I wouldn't say it felt like we were powerless. We were always trying to get something going but nothing would come for us. When a side is hungry like that the whole game, it's bloody hard to stop them especially when you can't do anything right. Everyone gets frustrated and goes quiet and they wait for someone else to do it. It's a great feeling when you're doing that to a side. It's just not so good when it's happening to you.

They knew they had us, too. They were all shouting. Tuqiri was giving us

Nothing needs to be said. It's all there to see from the guys on the bench to the rest of us on the field. The dream was over – again.

heaps and good on him. I would have done the same. You rub it when you have it over a side. I can't recall all the things they said but I know there was a hell of a lot of sledging going on, like George Gregan when he said to Byron Kelleher: "Don't worry boys. You've only got another four years to wait".

The worst thing is there was nothing you could say back to them – and they knew that. And that frustrates you the most because you know they're right. It happens all the time in games. I'll give plenty of cheek on the field when I know we have the ammunition to be able to do so. Everyone does the same.

I was in the same position myself when we faced the Crusaders in Christchurch

Here's yet another World Cup scoreboard New Zealand rugby followers don't want to remember.

in the second round of the 2004 Super 12. There we were leading 31–29 with time almost up when we attacked from our own goal-line and I backed up to score the last try. But rather than put the ball down as soon as I crossed the line, I deliberately headed right away from the posts because I wanted to chew up any time there might have been left – just to rub it in for all my friends in Christchurch. Of course, I enjoyed that. I'd be lying if I said I didn't. The Wallabies were just the same that night in Sydney.

In the most basic way, that semi-final was just one of those games, I'm afraid. No excuses, disappointment and plenty of it, but I would just as quickly say the Wallabies deserved a hell of a lot of credit for the job they did on us.

I found it difficult to isolate a player or a few of them who made the difference for them. The outside backs in Mortlock, Tuqiri and Sailor certainly gave them another dimension. They were like extra loose forwards but their whole unit was good.

The Wallabies celebrated the moment and so they should have. For us, there was only misery.

Defeat in big games like that eats away at you and afterwards in the dressing room there were plenty of us feeling that way. You can't explain what it's like in those moments. You sit in the room and think about the reasons why it happened – did we do this? Did we do that? If only we'd done that? They all start popping up in your own mind, in your own quiet time. You're feeling sorry for the whole team, everyone from management to the players involved on the night and the rest of the squad. Everyone was empty.

Mitch and Robbie Deans handled it as best they could. They told us they were just as disappointed as we were. I'm sure they were, too. It must have been as hard for them as anyone to talk to us after losing a semi-final at the World Cup, especially to a bunch of players who really weren't in any mood to hear anyone or anything.

It's a huge honour to play for your country. It's another one again to lead the haka.

CHAPTER 14

Jonny be Good

AFTER LOSING THE WORLD CUP SEMI-FINAL to the Aussies, we must have spent an hour and half in the dressing room drowning our sorrows, trying to stop sulking and having a shower. It takes about an hour to drag yourself up off your seat after an experience of that sort. We also went into the Wallabies' dressing room and had a bit of a drink with them to congratulate them. That's about the first time I could remember doing that and it was good to do it, too.

Richie McCaw, Justin Marshall and a few of the guys appeared for television interviews, which was a fairly gutsy effort on their part. It's not too easy fronting up when your World Cup has just finished. By the time we got on the bus it must have been after 11.00pm before we went back to the hotel and had a feed. After losing a World Cup semi-final, nothing else matters too much for the next few hours or days, or even weeks and months for some. I'm not in that camp. I'm a bit different. Even after that I found it quite easy to leave it behind me. It's a waste of energy if you don't.

But once the Wallabies had beaten us, the thought of playing again in a few days to decide third and fourth place still didn't exactly thrill any of us. We couldn't even wallow in the defeat with a decent team session, mainly because we had a quick turnaround from the semi-final on Saturday night to the play-off four days later.

Even worse, we actually had to return to Melbourne in between because all our bags were there. So we flew back there on Sunday, packed and flew back to Sydney on Tuesday. That was smart organisation, let me tell you. It was a nightmare week. Now, I love the World Cup. It's a great event and occasion, even though a little too much importance is attached to it in New Zealand at times.

What I can't see any need for, though, is this third-fourth match. Ever since the World Cup started, just about everyone has complained about it but we still have it. The thought of needing to play that match just a few days later was frustrating, which is putting it mildly. It's a nothing game, just a chance to make some more money with no real thought for the players.

It's the only question I'd have about the World Cup's format. If the motivation for having the match is to earn some more revenue from gate-takings and television rights, then why not have a game that actually has something on it. Third or fourth – who cares?

We were stuck with it. It's still a test and a game you want to win but after losing the semi-final, playing France was the last thing you felt like doing. Probably the only guys busting a gut to play in it would have been those who had seen little or no action at the World Cup. So, that game came and went without creating any interest at all. I couldn't tell you anything about it actually.

To me it would be better to have bowl and plate competitions running during the sudden-death phase of the tournament and having finals for those rather than a match to find third and fourth.

For the 2003 tournament, 20 teams were again involved, as they were in 1999. It means a lot of lesser rugby nations take part, countries like Namibia, Uruguay, Romania, Georgia and others. They're never going to worry the big boys.

Some thought has been given to having a second division competition alongside a contest for the top-ranked teams, in effect a tournament for the smaller nations. I don't agree with that. I think it still needs to be one tournament. I know they're in for heavy defeats but this is probably the only time a lot of countries will have the chance to play against New Zealand, England, Australia or South Africa so it's exciting for them. People might think there was no point Namibia playing the Wallabies but, despite being beaten 142-0, the Namibian players would have loved the chance to play against the defending world champions.

So, I'd like to see bowl and plate competitions running after the pool play just to keep some of the countries involved for a little bit longer, to give them something to play for. That's the way they do it at sevens tournaments and surely it could work at the World Cup as well. If there were bowl and plate finals, they could be played in the week leading up to the World Cup final, not even in the same city where the final is being staged. For the 2003 tournament they could have gone to Brisbane for one of them and Canberra, Perth or Melbourne for the other one. It's something that should be looked at.

Not that there was too much wrong with the 2003 tournament. It didn't work out well for the All Blacks. It didn't work out well for the New Zealand Rugby Union either when it lost the sub-hosting rights, although I actually think we were better off playing all our games in Australia in the end, rather than travelling backwards and forwards if we'd been a co-host. The Australians ran the event brilliantly.

And after the way the Wallabies beat us up, I couldn't see any reason why they wouldn't go on to beat England in the final. Beating us would have given the Aussies a huge confidence boost just when they needed it most. They knew they had a sniff.

If they'd played the same way against England they would have succeeded but the weather conditions never suited them. On a dry day the Aussies would have run the Poms' forwards around and they would have struggled. As it was, they did well even in the rain to take it all the way to extra time before Jonny Wilkinson's dropped goal beat them.

I always thought we could have beaten England if we'd had the chance but they still had a lot going for them. It wouldn't be fair to say they didn't. We knew they were going to be there – and I'm actually glad they won in the end, because the further the World Cup is away from this part of the world, the better. When it's over there I don't have to care about it as much!

All year England had been the most consistent side. They couldn't be denied

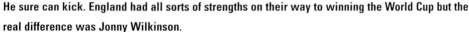

He sure can kick. England had all sorts of strengths on their way to winning the World Cup but the real difference was Jonny Wilkinson.

Fair play to England – no one should begrudge them winning the 2003 Rugby World Cup. All year they'd been the world's most consistent side.

that. The Rugby Union Players' Association had named the All Blacks as the team of the year just a few days before the World Cup final, which seemed kind of strange I suppose. That had something to do with the year under review not including the World Cup, which made it all even stranger, but really they were the team of the year.

I wouldn't begrudge England winning but it doesn't mean I enjoy the way they play the game. If they're capable of moving the ball – and apparently they are – then you don't see it very often. That's the result of having that big and old forward pack. If they were running from sideline to sideline they wouldn't last long so they have a game plan that suits their forward pack. I accept you have to play the way they do sometimes and when the circumstances require it I'll do that, too, but bugger doing it all the time.

Wilkinson isn't my sort of first five. I wouldn't want to be kicking penalties and dropped goals all day. That's the way it seems they like to play it. Good on them. It's the big difference between us and them.

I find our style of rugby far more exciting, it's the way we like to play and it's the way most people prefer the game to be played as well. I really don't believe New Zealanders want to see a game plan that revolves around a first-five kicking the ball all day. Of course, your approach depends on the personnel you have in your team and also the conditions you play in.

In the Northern Hemisphere they're used to playing in heavier and damp conditions so much of the time that the style of rugby has to be adapted to suit. Their mentality is to play a tighter game. They've grown up like that. It's bred in them. Sometimes they open it up, it doesn't work and they go back to what they know best. I believe it's easier to go from the wide game to the close one than it is going from close to wide, which is why they struggle when they try to change.

But do you think they care? Not when they've got the World Cup. They were able to go home to all the parades and the celebrations. When the World Cup was over, we just went our separate ways. We didn't travel home as a team, heading to our own home airports travelling in casual clothes, which evidently some people didn't think was quite right. You'd expect a reaction like that. People would be out to have a shot at us after we'd been knocked out of the World Cup. Probably no matter what we did for the next few weeks, nothing was going to be right.

I thought the way we went home individually was the right thing to do. The tournament was over, we'd lost and we had nothing to celebrate. It was holiday time for us then, the end of the season. If we'd won the cup it would have been different. We would have gone home together with the prize and we would have celebrated big-time. A tour around the country or whatever might have been put in place – basically what the Poms did.

After a disappointment like that, lots of issues emerged after the tournament about the way some areas of our campaign had been handled by management. One of them was the relationship with our sponsors. We learned later that there had been some matters there that had caused concern. The truth is we, as players, knew nothing of what was going on with that sort of thing. Whatever discussions there were between the NZRU, sponsors and our own management, we didn't know about it. We weren't told sponsors were keen to come in asking us to do some work with them. It was all kept from us. It's work that needs to be done and we'll do it when we're made aware of it.

With individual sponsorships whether it's with adidas or any other sponsor, then players also don't hesitate to fulfil commitments with them. They do that well but in a team environment it can be more difficult. From what I can gather, our management at the World Cup believed turning up for that sort of work would have been a distraction for us. But maybe it would have added some variety to our time. We'll never know.

To be honest, a lot of things that went on during and after the tournament washed over me. I had no idea at the time that Mitch had been told by NZRU CEO Chris Moller that his job was going to be advertised and that he'd have to reapply for it.

The truth was, once the World Cup was over, I dropped it out of my system. I didn't worry myself about issues like what might happen over the coaching or anything. My only real thoughts on the coaching at the time were that I thought Mitch had done enough to deserve another shot at it.

What I do know is the next World Cup tournament in 2007 will make it 20 years since New Zealand won the Webb Ellis Cup. Coaches, players and supporters have wanted success every time since then without achieving it. In fact, we've been in the final just one other time (1995) and have been beaten in the semi-finals three times.

So, is it a mental battle for us now because it's so long since we won it? Not for me. I don't let that sort of thing bother me. I'm sure the public sees it that way, that there is a psychological problem there now. Let's face it, 20 years will be a long time. If you have the chance as a player to win it for the country, then that's what you really want to do – to win the World Cup. If you don't do it, you feel you've let everyone down – yourself, your team-mates and the whole country.

I suppose the NZRU has to look ahead to each World Cup and plan for it for four years but sometimes I think we are too caught up in what it is and making all our plans for that one event. After the 2003 World Cup the discussions were all about trying to find a coach to last until the end of the 2007 World Cup. Hell, are we thinking about that already? That's how the NZRU probably has to approach it but for the players it's different. We don't think that far ahead, at least I don't. Anything might happen between now and then.

Many countries will look at a long-term coach to take a side through four years to include a World Cup. I don't see why it needs to be like that. There's nothing wrong with bringing in a coach two years before the event, maybe even later. There's a chance they could come in and freshen things up with new ideas. If you have respect for the man it doesn't matter how long he has been there as coach. If a coach came in just a matter of months before a World Cup and earned the players' respect just like that, then I don't see it being a problem.

Clive Woodward's been around a long time and now he has a World Cup. Rod Macqueen was in charge of the Wallabies for a decent stretch and he collected a World Cup in 1999. The South Africans have chopped and changed all over the place although Kitch Christie wasn't there long at all and he won.

If a coach is in charge for four years you'd imagine he must be doing a good job but to commit to a coach for that long can cause problems. I think the NZRU probably has it right with the arrangement for Graham Henry. This deal is for two years, which gives a chance for a review before going one way or the other for the next two years through to the World Cup.

I'd have to say, though, if this doesn't work with these coaches Ted (Graham Henry), Wayne Smith and Steve Hansen, then I don't know what would. I don't think you could bring together three better coaches in the world than those guys. This arrangement covers all options in terms of quality coaches and it also provides a mix of people from Auckland and Canterbury, which can't be a bad thing, and there's also a manager (Darren Shand) from Canterbury. Even my friends from around Christchurch must approve.

We're very lucky because all three coaches have been overseas, broadening their outlook on how to do their job. All three have also coached international sides – Henry with Wales and the Lions, Hansen taking over from him with Wales and Smith as All Black coach in 2000-01. They know what it's all about.

I'm not sure whether it's an absolute must for All Black coaches to have overseas experience but the way the rugby world has developed, with England going ahead the way they have, it must be an advantage. In the case of the coaches the

Moving on from the 2003 World Cup, Graham Henry was appointed coach and he brought in Steve Hansen (centre) and Wayne Smith (right) as his assistants. I couldn't have imagined a better combination.

All Blacks have now, it has exposed them to different styles of rugby and working with other nationalities. That must benefit them and you'd hope it benefits us as well.

If these guys can't make it work in the short or medium term, then something's wrong. As a rugby nation, I think New Zealanders are prepared to let a new coach settle in. It's nice to have immediate success but the general reaction is to cut a bit of slack before raising expectations ahead of the next World Cup.

I know I don't even want to think as far ahead as 2007. That's too far off for me to consider in any depth. Just let me worry about the rest of 2004 first and then I might start to give 2005 a bit of thought. I'll be happy enough in 2007 if I'm still as quick as I am now. I'll be 31 then, rising 32, and in my prime! Thinking about having another shot at the World Cup is the

Canterbury's Darren Shand, the new All Black manager in 2004.

last thing on my mind but at least I have played at one World Cup now after missing out in 1999.

Once the 2003 experience was finally all over, Jodene and I flew to Noosa on Australia's Sunshine Coast to kick back, put rugby aside and move on. By the time we arrived home, there didn't appear to be too much ill-feeling about what had happened against the Wallabies. I actually found fans fairly generous, saying the semi-final was a shame but they were generally complimentary. It was nothing like what happened after the 1999 World Cup when there was a feeling of hatred basically. It was an odd reaction which I couldn't quite figure out because in '99 the All Blacks were actually in contention against France and they were just bagged that much – or at least John Hart was – after it. That was totally unwarranted. We weren't really in it at all in Sydney but we weren't given that much of a rough time at all.

I wasn't going to let it bother me at all over the summer. All I could think about was the old advice of getting back on the horse. We'd taken a bit of a dumping but at least, as players, we could rip straight back into playing rugby in 2004. That's the great thing about it. There's always another game of rugby just around the corner, a new chance to start all over again, to worry about what you can do right now and leave the past where it belongs – in the past.

CHAPTER 15

Sticking Around

T HERE ARE PLENTY OF TIMES in life when things don't run quite the way you'd like them to and that seems to happen a lot when your job is a fairly public one like that of a professional rugby player. Different coaches have different opinions on where each player figures in their plans, which is only natural. That's just part of the game really. At the same time, it can be a bit unsettling for players. That's certainly how I felt in 2002.

I guess you start questioning your value. If I'm not cutting it with a certain coach, is it any use sticking around? It's easy to say you should harden up but decisions by coaches and selectors have a big bearing on careers. One moment you're in, the next you're out and that takes a bit of getting used to. I try not to let it affect me too much but I'm not a machine.

So, the All Black selectors had made it clear through the early internationals in 2002 and then the Tri Nations that I, along with a lot of Auckland players, wasn't in their plans. That was their call and, on its own, would be the cause for great argument. Everyone has their own view. For me, though, this seemed to follow John Mitchell's comments that he thought I was a fullback, not a first five-eighth.

When you are overlooked for higher honours, it always brings out overseas interest and, at this time, I had a few approaches for a commitment at the end of my current contract which expired after the 2003 Air New Zealand NPC. The approaches certainly interested me although the further the 2002 season went, the more I wanted to stay in New Zealand. First there was Auckland's win in the 2002 NPC and that in turn earned a recall to the All Blacks for their end of year tour to England, Wales and France. Of course, I was excited about that but any decision to remain in New Zealand would still have to be based on being able to

negotiate suitable contract terms with the New
Zealand Rugby Union and the Auckland Rugby
Union. The Auckland rugby people, especially
through the efforts of chief executive David White,
were keen that I stayed on after 2003 and went all
out to help to put something together for me.

That was only part of it, though. There was also
the business of dealing with the NZRU. We had to
work through a few issues and at times this was
quite demanding but the Auckland union have
been incredibly supportive. They have played a
huge role in keeping me in New Zealand and I
thoroughly appreciate everything they've done for
me over the past six years. They've come to the
party big-time and have always looked after me.

**Auckland Rugby Union chief
executive David White.**

DOJ: *"David White and the Auckland union were acutely aware Carlos was
under attack from overseas late in 2002. They realised he was susceptible to
approaches after the way he'd been overlooked in All Black selection decisions in the
previous two years. Because Auckland wanted to renew their contract with Carlos,
we had to find out what the NZRU were prepared to do. The NZRU weren't particularly enthusiastic. They were prepared to re-contract him but with a salary cut –
and they did cut it, by 25 per cent.*
*"On one hand they were saying they wanted to keep him but on the other they
seemed to suggest that he was not that important to them. The attitude to him
seemed to be similar to that displayed in 2000 following his World Cup 1999
injury. It was the same attitude which led Carlos to two periods of self-examination
in which he questioned whether staying in New Zealand was in his best interests."*

I don't know what it is with the New Zealand Rugby Union. I haven't been
able to figure out where I sit in the order of things when it comes to my contract.
I've had a few issues with the NZRU over the last couple of years in the way they
look after players but there's not a lot I can do. I've just got to keep trucking.
There's only so much we can do as players, and so much we can ask for. If they've
made up their mind about something, there's not a lot we can do about it, no matter how unfair it might seem. You can accept your lot – which I usually do – and
just get on with it, or pack your bag and go, which I've just about done.

On balance, of course I'm still happy I'm in New Zealand. I could have jacked
it all in and gone overseas but here is where I'd prefer to be. The other advantage
in that for me now – and especially now – is that I'm able to set myself up in a

business sense. If I was in England for a few years I wouldn't be able to do much in terms of establishing my life after rugby unless I was going to do so over there and stay there. This way in my last few years of playing rugby here, I can make those arrangements without any problems. An overseas offer would have to be good to give up the lifestyle I have here but there has always been quite a challenge in coming to terms with the NZRU.

> **DOJ:** *"Given the NZRU's salary proposals for a renewed contract to 2006, David White and the Auckland Rugby Union had a bit of a challenge to keep Carlos. They needed to find someone (a sponsor) to fill the gap, or make up the difference themselves. Even then, that would only put Carlos' salary back to the point it was at before the NZRU had cut his pay.*
> *"These are the difficulties Carlos has to deal with. Auckland rugby people value him. They've been very good, especially David White. The other group which values him very highly are the overseas clubs. He has consistently been more valued overseas than any other player I know. During the 2004 Super 12 season I received a huge unsolicited offer for him. It was massive and there hadn't been any approach or negotiation at all by Carlos. And that was an offer for the end of the 2005 season.*
> *"Auckland have been so good in this whole process. They came through and did the deal to keep him here. If it wasn't for Auckland's proactive response, I believe Carlos would have gone."*

While David White and the Auckland union did a lot for me, the man who actually made it work was businessman Balu Khan, who's a strong supporter of Auckland rugby. As part of the deal, I would do some work for Balu in what is an endorsement contract, joining him at some business meetings or events in a promotional capacity. If it wasn't for him, Auckland would have needed to find the money required and I don't know whether that would have been possible. I've got so much to thank Balu for but also the ARU for sticking with me.

The options in 2006 will be to sign again for one last shot at the World Cup, if everything's running well – and if I'm still functioning – or to consider an overseas contract. That's a long way off to think about and I don't want to consider it right now. I'm stretched enough to think about rugby day by day.

But once the hassle of my new contract was out of the way, my mind was set on doing what I enjoy most – playing rugby in New Zealand, and doing so through to the end of 2006. Everyone involved in the World Cup basically had the chance to do just that in the 2004 Super 12. For the Blues, there was every reason to be optimistic about it, too. We'd had a brilliant run in 2003, and in 2004, we had fairly much the same squad and coaches although with one notable difference – Graham Henry was no longer with us, of course.

Plenty of people thought we were the surest things to win the title again, and to even go through unbeaten. There was nothing wrong with anyone saying that or thinking it either. Why not? We had a good enough side as long as we played up to our ability and we also gave ourselves the best possible preparation with three build-up matches, all of which we won. We didn't feel cocky or anything after that. We just felt ready. I know I was dead keen to be back playing rugby. The 2003 Rugby World Cup? What was that? It wasn't even on my mind. I'd long since forgotten about it.

But if we thought we were ready we soon discovered we weren't when the Brumbies tore straight into us in the first round in Canberra and it's fair to say our campaign probably never held together that well from then on.

I felt confident enough myself and had the chance to be reasonably involved in the match, especially in the first half but we had obvious problems up front all night. Our ball retention wasn't good at all, our set pieces weren't at the level we expected of ourselves and we suffered.

The Brumbies played the way we wanted to play. They got all their set pieces right while we didn't have possibly even half of ours right; they stole our lineout ball, we didn't steal any of theirs so we were on the back foot all night. I told the boys at halftime that we were lucky to be 20-all. It should have been 20-0 to them to be honest. We managed to stick in there for about 60 minutes on scrappy ball but then the Brumbies went on with it.

Our tries were basically scored off scraps. We had no continuous supply of ball, therefore no momentum and that was the end of it. We lost 27-44 and we deserved to lose. It was amazing we stayed in contention for as long as we did. While it wasn't such a good night for us I don't think any of us guessed then that our campaign would be in a fair bit of trouble very soon.

Before we could think too much about what went wrong in Canberra, we were into a rematch of the 2003 Super 12 final – same opposition but different venue. Like us, the Crusaders had opened their season unsatisfactorily after being stuffed by the Waratahs. Having the Brumbies and the Crusaders as our first two opponents for the year was fairly demanding but we had to work with it.

I loved this game against the Crusaders. The atmosphere down there was great and, as for the football, it's amazing what a difference a reasonable supply of possession makes. We had it in this game and ended up having a great night. Rupeni (Caucaunibuca) had three tries and I finished with a couple as well in a match I might well remember a bit longer than most – and it's not my style to do that.

The Crusaders got stuck into us early but we stayed in there with a bit of long-range football. We had a lot of kickable penalties in that match but between us, Rushie (Xavier Rush) and I favoured the set play option every time. We just felt we had a really good chance of scoring five-pointers whenever we were deep on attack.

Once the 2004 Super 12 came around the World Cup was well forgotten, especially after having a bit of fun for the Blues against the Crusaders.

There was only one penalty later in the match that I wasn't so sure about. We were leading 31-29 and I thought we should have a shot to take us out to a five-point lead. Rushie decided to go for the scrum, arguing a try would put the match out of reach where a penalty would still put us only five points ahead. I supported him on that – only it didn't work out that time. If we'd gone for the penalty, they'd kick off, they could have claimed the ball gone down to our end to score a try and convert and they still would have won it.

All the commentators were saying: "Stupid." Mate, you're not on the field. We think of other things as well. That's the way we are. We didn't score a try as it happened from that decision but that's the way it goes. We had a shot at it. Hell, that night we scored six tries to their three so we must have done something right.

The Crusaders kept threatening and had a chance with a dropped goal and a penalty to take the lead, only to miss. Then inside the last couple of minutes, Caleb

One of my more satisfying nights had to be the Blues' win over the Crusaders at Jade Stadium in Christchurch in the 2004 Super 12.

Ralph was a real show to score a try that would have won it – but knocked on.

That's when the fun started. I asked the ref Paddy O'Brien how much time there was to go and he told me there was a minute and half left. So we had a scrum just a few metres out. If there had been less time left, my only thought would have been to put the ball into touch from the scrum but because there was 90 seconds I thought there was enough time for the Crusaders to win it if I went for touch. They'd have the lineout throw and time to set themselves up for a dropped goal or something.

I figured we needed to keep hold of the ball for a minute. Rushie took it off the back of the scrum. My first instinct would have been to work back towards the forwards, to keep the ball with them but I saw their backs racing up so I thought I could kick it long right or shift it. They made up my mind for me.

I could see Joe (Rokocoko) was open so I hurled a high pass out to my right, intentionally high to get over the advancing defenders – and despite what people said afterwards, no, it wasn't in danger of hitting the goalposts. It wasn't even close. Joe would have seen the long pass was on because their second five-eighth and centre rushed up on ours. If I got the pass over the top of them and into his arms he was away.

And that's how it happened. Joe charged off up-field and Justin Collins did incredibly well to take off to back him up, take the pass and then off-load to me. From there I just had a run to the line – but that's when it became really exciting.

As I got close to the line I instantly thought I should do all I could to waste more time, to chew up the clock and ensure there wasn't the slightest chance for the Crusaders. I knew I was going to score so, as I was heading towards the line I thought: "I'll run the clock out. I'll take it to sideline and take my time dotting down." In the end there were a whole lot of Blues players around me and none from the Crusaders. Paddy O'Brien was peering through legs to see whether I'd forced the ball and the guys couldn't afford to touch me until I had.

Apparently people thought I was mad because I made the conversion so difficult and if I didn't get it that would have given the Crusaders a bonus point. I've heard since that one of the radio commentators said I had behaved like a dickhead – before I'd taken the conversion. I'll take that as a compliment. I'm quite surprised I have that sort of effect on people that they feel the need to call me names. It's so good that something so small annoys them. And the TV commentators went on as well about what would happen if I missed the kick – well, the kick didn't miss. End of the story.

I enjoyed the game but I wouldn't go so far as to say it was one of the most satisfying I'd been involved in. First and foremost it was a win we needed after beginning with a loss to the Brumbies and, in all honesty, it was just another round-robin game in the Super 12. Nothing more than that, although it was nice to be able to give my Christchurch supporters something they enjoyed so much.

They always like to be a little bit provocative down there. It wouldn't be right if they weren't. I'd certainly be wondering what's wrong with them. Then again, there are people like that all over the place, rugby fans who think they're better than anyone. It's good to get in among the people, though. It doesn't make us lock ourselves away and look for private bars to drink in, not even in Christchurch. You wouldn't let the people down there stop you having a good time. I love going out for a few drinks down there and that night it felt a bit better than usual.

When you do that you usually end up the target of abuse from the odd bogan. I just ignore it. Usually it's because they've had too much to drink. But that's all part of it, just as crowd abuse is during games. Some of it you hear, some of it you don't. Some are funny, clever. Some aren't. That's fine. You live with them all. It's part of being a rugby player. These guys are always a minority and the fans are usually pretty good to us.

In the same way players have lots of verbals thrown at them, they're also under more scrutiny than ever in terms of behaviour in public. There've been a few incidents with players over the years, not too many. When we're out the rule is to make sure we all look after each other. Everyone's basically fairly good despite the odd case where someone has too much and regrets it the next day, or someone finds out about it. Guys have to be careful because there are people out there looking whereas when I first came up to Auckland in 1994 no one really cared too much what you did when you were out on the town. You could get away with anything but not now since the word professional has come into it. Everyone's after you now. Most guys know when they've had enough.

One week I was celebrating, the next I was on the bench after breaking my jaw in the Blues' loss to the Chiefs.

Having enjoyed the game and the night in Christchurch, we might have thought we had the show back in better shape. Unfortunately that was one of the few high points for us during the Super 12 because, just a week later, our season started to hit more than a bit of trouble when the Chiefs beat us at Eden Park for the first time, winning 27-20 on the back of Sione Lauaki's last-second try.

That wasn't just a bad night for us but it was also a fairly miserable one for me personally when I had my jaw broken in a heavy collision with Chiefs prop Deacon Manu. It was just one of those things that can happen in football. You can't do anything about it and I didn't have any complaints.

It happened just on halftime and I knew something wasn't right. After that I didn't even know what was going on. I was in some pain and I was also dazed. I went back out in the second half but can't remember anything, not even putting through a kick for Dougy (Howlett) to score. Midway through the second half I was taken off and I gave the impression of not being too pleased about it. Peter Sloane had made the move in the interests of my own welfare and, while I didn't know it then, I later realised there was no way I could have stayed on.

I needed surgery to have two plates inserted on the right side of my jaw, an injury that put me out for a month. That was frustrating enough but the worst part was that I couldn't do much in the way of training and I was also on a soft diet for three to four weeks. That was really annoying. As well as that, it was taking me half an hour to eat when usually it takes me five minutes.

After that loss, things got a lot worse. We were beaten by the Reds at Ballymore – we still haven't beaten them there – and drew with the Hurricanes. I was able to return against the Waratahs, a match we won but did little that was impressive before we had a really big night beating the Bulls 56-19. We had a lot of fun in that game when lots of things came off.

But then a week later we had a real shocker against the Stormers when they

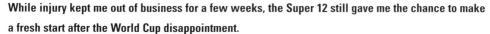

While injury kept me out of business for a few weeks, the Super 12 still gave me the chance to make a fresh start after the World Cup disappointment.

swamped us. I've certainly had better nights than that one. The fact we then won both games in South Africa against the Cats and the Sharks plus our final round-robin match against the Highlanders back at home weren't enough to enable us to sneak into the top four. We didn't need anyone else to tell us where we'd gone wrong. This was simply a campaign that never got into gear, especially up front in the first half of the competition.

The question could be asked about how much Ted's absence hurt us. I don't know. He was so helpful in 2003 with his defensive work and analysis and I suppose it must have made quite a difference not having him around in 2004.

Still, he had more important matters to consider in his position as All Black coach. As soon as the Super 12 was over, he had his mind set on an All Black trial. We hadn't had one of those for a few years so for most of the players it was a new experience. John Hart was a coach who liked trials and it was under him that we'd last had one in 1998, not that I can remember playing in it – but I did apparently. Six years later I was doing it all over again, only this time the man in charge was the coach who'd done so much to start my career at the highest level and now I wanted to be part of his All Black team.

And the winners were . . . the Brumbies. They deserved their Super 12 success in 2004, dominating the final.

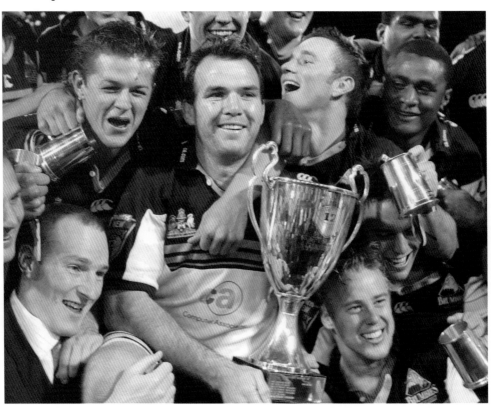

A Pro's Life

FOR NINE YEARS NOW we've had this sporting life, this one of being paid to play the game of our choice. That form teacher I had at Waiopehu College never thought it was possible – and I'd have to admit I didn't imagine it could quite work out this way either when I left Levin for Auckland in 1994.

Then again, no one really expected the face of the game to change quite as swiftly as it did in 1995, opening the way for what we enjoy today. I'm always grateful for that. How could I not be?

Sometimes I wonder what it would have been like to have a so-called normal job, like the one I started with on first arriving in Auckland. I don't stop to think about it for long because I don't need to. This is my normal job. I've been privileged to be in this position and I want to do all I can to ensure it continues for just a little while longer yet.

I'm sure there's an impression that pro rugby players don't have all that much to do. We have it fairly easy with a bit of training and then a game – that's all, isn't it? Well, there's probably a bit more to it than that in what can be an odd existence with our plans changing a lot. The nature of things means we do have time available during any day of what might be called our working week but there's not always a lot of what I'd call spare time or quality time so you can switch off for a few hours.

When there is, I like nothing more than heading off for a ride on my bike and taking things easy. I had a fascination with motorbikes all those years ago in Levin and I've been able to do something about it. I've now got a 2003 Harley-Davidson Deuce that's been fairly much rearranged. I've changed the tank, guards, wheels and bars so it's a much different bike than it was in its original shape. Just

about all I've kept are the engine and the frame.

So, when I can, I blast around wherever I feel like going, taking off for a good couple of hours, maybe out towards Bombay south of Auckland or out towards Piha and Muriwai. I try to find somewhere with a bit of open road so I can have a nice cruise. You just don't have a worry out there when you're riding, apart from watching out for the traffic, of course.

There's an older guy down the road from me who also has a Harley and every now and then we'll go out for a cruise together. Cashy (Adrian Cashmore) used to have a Harley and he and I would do a bit of riding as well. It's so good to do – and so far, no accidents either thankfully. Hopefully it will stay that way but you never know when they might come with bikes. I haven't been picked up speeding either... not yet! To be honest, I'm sensible. You have to be. I have the bike just to cruise on, not to be stupid on.

Relaxation and other outlets outside rugby become important in professional sport. You soon realise you need them just to break up your programme. I don't just mean amusement either. It could be some other form of work, an interest or perhaps business pursuits, which are coming into the picture more and more for me these days.

Often it's something with a sporting connection, I guess. Golf seemed to be the most obvious thing to do as pro rugby was first starting and there used to be quite a few of us who were interested in playing as much as we could. Although it was never that easy fitting in a round of golf between training sessions, we'd get out on courses a lot. Maybe we've tended to realise as we've matured that there's a bit more to life than running off to a golf course every time we have the chance but in 1996 Robin Brooke, Junior Tonu'u, Charlie Riechelmann, Zinzan Brooke, Mark Carter and I were more than keen to squeeze in a round somewhere whenever there was an opening. I used to swing a club reasonably well, too, but haven't been so hot more recently. Back then I was good enough to enjoy a decent round, and to make a bit of money here and there as well, or win a couple of lunches. We were always playing for something. Time's always the problem with golf and it's lapsed a bit lately. We try to get out once every three weeks or so now but usually it just doesn't happen that much anymore.

Away from rugby and the boys, Jodene and I like to take things easy. Occasionally we'll catch a movie and I'm typical of a lot of blokes who like action movies more so, like a bit of Arnie. Give me the fighting and killing with a bit of blood and guts in it including a good war movie. Every now and then I need to go for one of the hand-holding ones that bring out the tears just to balance things

Opposite: One of my prized possessions is my Harley-Davidson Deuce. Going for a blast is the best way to get away from it all.

up – and I actually don't mind them, provided they have decent storylines.

Generally Jodene and I are more likely to head out to dinner rather than a movie. Well, that's the way it used to be until a little bit of company arrived on April 23, 2004, in the shape of our son Payton Cruz. He changes the daily flow of life just a bit.

Before he came along, Jodene was working full-time so, if we couldn't be bothered cooking, we'd eat out. That's about it for us in the course of a normal week and when breaks, long weekends or holidays come along we're usually making tracks for our place at the beach on the Coromandel Peninsula or we go away somewhere else, like back home to Levin to see Mum and Dad, family and friends down there.

The beach is my real favourite. It's just awesome to be able to spend time down there, to chill out and get away from everything but it's not possible when we're in season with our football. There are even fewer windows of opportunity since the game went professional because so much more of your time is committed.

Whether it's going away – when you can – having a ride on the bike, a game of golf, taking in a movie or dinner or maybe just having an afternoon doze, they're all aspects that provide both variety and balance, which we all need in our lives whatever we do. It's just so important in professional sport to ensure you stay fresh both physically and mentally.

Central to everything and every day is my diet. Much as I enjoy training, nothing's more critical to me than food. I'm always eating. I need something in my stomach at all times; if I don't, I get tired and just lose energy so quickly. So, before ripping into a day's work, breakfast kicks me off with something like cornflakes, bananas and some fruit salad plus a protein shake (and I'd have about three or four of them a day).

Most of the boys are like me. We like our food and lots of it. Often a barbecue will be put on after training. On the days when lunch isn't served, there's time between the two training sessions and usually I like to go home for lunch.

Most of the time, it's a personal responsibility to keep an eye on what you eat. The only time there's a real control over our intake is when we're all staying together before a match. When we assemble on a Thursday night for a Friday night game, the food will cover all requirements – proteins, carbohydrates, vitamins. All you need.

A lot of guys will still have a big breakfast and a big lunch on the day of a night game with lunch on offer about three hours before the match. Some guys don't like eating too much at all leading up to a match. It's just what works best for them. Food's always available for you if you need it.

When it comes down to it, though, the focus of a pro rugby player's life isn't on what he'd like to eat or do but on what he has to do – training and playing. One aspect of rugby that has changed dramatically and evolved is the attitude to

Professional football life can be a bit of a treadmill but I never tire of training. It suits me just fine.

off-season and pre-season training. When we were heading into the first years of the Super 12, my recollection is that we had little in the way of training in the off-season. We did nothing at all before Christmas and didn't really come back together as a squad until almost the end of January. We'd have only five or six weeks and then we'd be into the Super 12.

Now our off-season training is fairly similar to what happens with the rugby league boys in the NRL. In fact, it's modelled a lot on what they've been doing for years.

Once our home season is over – that is after the Air New Zealand NPC – we have four weeks off and then we come back for some work before Christmas. A week or so short of Christmas Day, we break off again and reassemble early in January. The exception is those players who might have an end of year All Black tour, in which case you have four weeks off after returning home from the tour and come back to training after that.

I love the training. You have to if you want to survive in this game now. It's a struggle if you hate training because there's a hell of a lot of it. I'm not so hot on the running element. I'm keener on the drills and working with the ball as well as weights. We've got the facilities for that at Eden Park now, with a gym there and all.

The attention now paid to off-season training has also resulted in big changes in the body shape of rugby players. Forwards, especially, never used to have much muscle definition at all. Most of them were just slabs. You could get away with that because no one in rugby was doing weights, or very, very few were. Now you have to because everyone's into it. You'll get left behind if you don't.

The emphasis and type of training naturally varies depending on whether we're out of season or in-season but when we're at work at any time of the year we operate from a schedule mapped out each week. It's usually handed to us every Monday outlining our training programme right down to what each session will revolve around. It can change from time to time but not too much.

With all this training, usually twice a day, living in a city like Auckland means a fair bit of the time in between can be taken up travelling to and from training plus eating, resting or maybe doing some jobs around home like cleaning, vacuuming or buying groceries. Surprised at me doing that? You shouldn't be. I'm a new-age man, a multi-tasker. It's a reminder that we are more than just professional footballers.

So what can you expect on a daily basis? Well, heading into the 2004 season, a typical week for a working footballer associated with the Blues looked a bit like this...

MONDAY

First stop to begin the week is a gym session, the forwards at 9.30 and the backs jumping in at 10.00. It's great to have a gym at Eden Park now, something we didn't have until the new stand was built. It's a good facility with just about the only things missing being a plunge pool and a couple of spas. The gym sessions run for about an hour to an hour and a half. Early in the season, the focus is on power and strength work.

After that, it's home for lunch. The gap between sessions – when we have two a day – might be around three hours, which sounds like a reasonable amount of time but, with the way traffic is in Auckland it might not be that long at all, especially for guys who have to travel to the North Shore.

If I go home I try to play the good boy helping around the house. We've also got two bulldogs that need a bit of looking after – Sarj, who's about three years old and Diesel, who's not even one. I used to have a bull mastiff but I've since found bulldogs have a great nature and are really good with kids.

A pro's life might be a team run one session, strength work the next and whiteboard work as well. There's plenty of variety.

While going home to see the dogs and do some jobs is an option, finding lunch isn't always a worry because it's regularly put on for us after training, maybe in the shape of a barbecue. The reason why it's done that way is because there's a concern some players can't be bothered going home to make themselves a decent lunch and opt to buy takeaways instead. This way, if something's put on after training, we know everyone has a good feed – decent food, not airy-fairy stuff – instead of eating rubbish. Then everyone can go home to have a rest or take care of things they need to attend to.

Takeaways aren't banned and I don't mind them myself, especially if I'm on the run. In that case I'll drop in and buy five burgers from McDonald's. That's right, five burgers. I chomp through that many easily. That would fill me up and give me some protein, especially after a hard training session. You can afford that when you're working really hard.

With lunch out of the way, we're back together for a training run in the afternoon. In the early part of the year, when cricket's still going at Eden Park, we use the Auckland Rugby League's facilities at Cornwall Park actually. The set-up's great there.

Head down and follow through . . . practising my kicking is important to me at any time.

I like to turn up maybe half an hour to 45 minutes early so I can have a bit of a play around with a ball, do some kicking and try a few tricks. The session starts about 3.00 and runs through to about 4.00. We start with stretching as team.

For the session, we might split into two sides and run our moves against the other side. One side is attack, one defence. We go over our game plan and different options. We always look for new ideas, trying to change things around because opposition sides soon pick up what you're doing.

We go over our themes. Basically we have four of them for different parts of the field and we keep working on them, maybe half a dozen times each. We're dealing with our options from set pieces, when we're expected to have possession and also when we're not, say a lineout win against the throw. We do that for a good hour, stopping to chat only if we feel something's not working and we need to stop to talk it through.

Obviously when new players come into the team, it can be a little more time-consuming at first trying to work them into the pattern, providing pointers about what we try to do, where we do it and how we do it, plus learning the calls, of course. For me that would apply especially to a new halfback or second five. Then I need to show them what I do.

So around 4.00 it's home again through Auckland's traffic, have a sit down for a while and some dinner, watch a bit of TV, get on to the computer downstairs, check my emails on my website, reply to messages on the message board and get in the spa about 9.00. After the spa I need to cool down for about half an hour before turning in for the night.

TUESDAY

We're doing intervals in the morning, starting at 9.30. There are two groups, one doing sets over a certain distance and the group I'm in does 12 sets of 50 metres, sprint 50, jog 50, 40 seconds rest and then into another 50. If one person lags and lets everyone else down, we all have to do an extra 50m sprint. We have a couple of minutes to rest after those and then we rip into another 12 of the same thing.

After that the backs and forwards split and we each run through a few organisational things like our calls. We change the calls from year to year, even during the season, because they get picked up fairly quickly. Players who were with us one season move to other teams and they know what we're up to so we have to keep everyone guessing. We need to keep them simple, though. After all, the forwards have to remember them and understand them and that's asking a lot. Calls can be really confusing for the forwards so we can't afford to let them get lost.

A lot of our calls might have names of other unions around New Zealand. We keep it fairly local. We might have shoe brands or boot brands as well or a clothing brand. We go over and over the calls and the moves just so everyone knows automatically what we're up to trying to steer ourselves around the field.

In these sessions our coaches Peter Sloane and Bruce Robertson are fairly standoffish. They let the guys run it and step in when they think they need to. They'll blow it up when they want to.

Rushie (Xavier Rush), Gus (Justin Collins) and I are some of the voices most heard I guess. Rushie's certainly a vocal captain. You hear him and you know what he wants. We all listen to him. He's a good leader.

At this stage of the year, we don't get into too much in the way of whiteboard sessions until the season's under way. It's best to keep whiteboard stuff fairly limited. It's easier working things out on the field, walking through things so everyone understands and feels comfortable.

After that session the afternoon's free, except for a group of us involved in an adidas shoot, a Super 12 commercial that takes a couple of hours at Cornwall Park. In the backs there's David Gibson, Sam Tuitupou, Ben Atiga and me and in the forwards Ali Williams, Kees Meeuws, Tony Woodcock, Bradley Mika and Jerome

Kaino. All I have to do is stand there. It isn't too stressful. It's a fun type of commercial rather than one of those staunch ones. They can be a bit of a pain. Then again it has to be done and you have to bear with the production people but it requires a fair bit of patience.

The shoot finished, I head home to have a look at a couple of houses. We're in the market for something else. No luck, though. I'm working through that with real estate agents.

That night we go out to dinner in St Heliers. I only like restaurants that serve decent-sized meals, not that pretty stuff you get a lot of the time. Heck, I need a plate with lots of food on it not something that's just about empty.

If there's a good late movie on TV I'll stay up and watch it, otherwise I'm probably in bed around 10.00.

WEDNESDAY

I'm up at 7.00, my normal rising time and into another day. But this one's different. It's not just hosing down. It's not just bucketing down. It's like a tidal wave out of the sky. It's forecast to be 23 degrees and to clear. Can't believe it will – but it does. And just in time for a fairly special session we're having. We're getting together with the New Zealand Warriors who are also well-advanced in their pre-season training regime heading towards the National Rugby League season.

This has been set up for a while. The Blues and the Warriors also had a session pre-Christmas after the 2002 season but I missed that one and so did a lot of the team because we were with the All Blacks touring England, France and Wales. Same thing with the Warriors. They were without a lot of their players who were touring Britain and France with the Kiwis at the time.

I've met quite a few of the Warriors out and about before, in bars and at functions and things. It wouldn't have happened even a few years ago but no one bothers about the union and league codes getting together now. Not too long after this one, Graham Henry, in his role as the new All Black coach, was invited to watch the Warriors train by their then-coach Daniel Anderson. Ted went along to check a few defensive ideas. It all makes a lot of sense.

The session we have with the Warriors is really good, really enjoyable. It's something so different and that's what we like. We've got some tall boys in the forwards, a lot taller than the league boys but they have some big boys, though. Really solid builds. Stacey Jones is there but isn't training.

We do some ball drills together plus some skills work and finish off with a couple of games before they run through a defensive drill with us. We go for about an hour. It's good to be involved with them.

Rugby league and rugby union side by side . . . then-Warriors coach Daniel Anderson and Graham Henry compare notes. It's the way it should be.

I haven't done a close study of what similarities there might be in the way the two games are played these days. It's true as a first five I now try to run to the line a lot, which I didn't do that much in the past and most first fives didn't do it at all. With such flat defensive lines in operation with the laws the way they are, first fives have a need to take on the line more to bring in runners. Tasesa Lavea can do it because he had a background in league with the Kiwis and the Melbourne Storm before returning to rugby union and Sammy Tuitupou's right into smashing into the defensive line as well: "Here, Sam – have this!" I just throw him the ball and he doesn't blink. He, too, has a bit of a league history.

The Mad Butcher puts on a barbecue and we mingle and have a feed. It's been a good day.

I head home to do some interviewing for my book for a couple of hours before going back to Eden Park for a stretching session, working on all muscle groups. I like to concentrate on the lower part of my body, my back and my quads. It's optional. Some guys do Pilates.

My legs haven't been too bad during my career. I had a hamstring tear once that kept me out for a bit and the knee reconstruction, of course, after being put out of the 1999 Rugby World Cup. I've also had shin splints and compartment syndrome, when the muscles go all hard, rock hard. Otherwise I've survived okay.

I have a massage, head home and have dinner. One thing I do little of during a regular week is having a drink. In fact, I wouldn't have a beer at all unless I catch up with some mates for a few. Otherwise I stay off it other than a glass of red wine if we go out to dinner. We don't have any team rules about not drinking during the week. I just don't feel like it. That's the only reason.

What I do feel like most nights is my spa. I don't miss out on that too often.

THURSDAY

Our morning training session focuses on speed work – one-on-one drills with the backs and forwards working separately. It's all dodging and weaving, stepping and swerving at speed. You're running with the ball and being chased. Tackle bag drills? Don't do much of that, only as part of our warm-ups.

The schedule varies from week to week, but leading up to a match – unless it's a Friday night one – Thursday can involve two training sessions. Maybe one will be based on speed work in the morning, the type of work we do being mixed up so the guys don't get bored. It might be trying to beat guys in one-on-one drills done at speed while the forwards might be working with sleds behind them. With the backs, we concentrate on short and explosive work.

Otherwise the session might revolve around the forwards doing some live scrummaging and lineouts. When that happens, the backs go off and work on some of our moves.

By the afternoon session on a Thursday – for a Saturday night game – we do more team stuff, a genuine team run before a light run on Friday morning when we go over everything just to make sure everyone's clear about what we're doing.

When we do our team sessions, the beauty of it when you have big squads is that we can do it against 15 players, or close to it. With injuries always a factor it's not often that it can be 15 on 15 but we're not too far off most times. It's not high intensity, fairly passive really but the concentration is on our organisation and our system with the players up against us providing a bit of defensive pressure.

FRIDAY

The schedule calls for weights in a window from 8.30 to 10.30. We go any time during that period to do our work. Early in the season I work mainly on strength.

In the afternoon it's an activity or team bonding day. Fishing has been lined up, heading out to a spot somewhere out there on the Hauraki Gulf – I couldn't possibly tell you where – that Geoff Thomas knows about. He takes us out there. We have a sensational afternoon catching something like 70 snapper. Some of the guys

Never forget your stretching. It's such an important part of any training session, both before it and after it. Same thing with every match.

catch five or six each. How good is that?

This is one thing that doesn't have a competitive element to it. This is leisure. For once we're not split into teams trying to outdo each other but we're always looking to give guys grief for catching the smallest fish, or none at all.

Geoff's always happy to get the boys out and have a couple of quiet beers. Everyone has to go out on afternoon activities of this type, which usually means a party of around 40 people all up. After the trip, some of us go around to Steve Devine's place to gut and fillet all the fish, put a few on the barbie and have a good feed.

Sometimes our manager Ant (Strachan) might be involved in organising something like this, or some of our off-field leaders will take care of it. We're always looking for activities to do away from the rugby field, something with a bit of fun involved.

With no game on this weekend and the Super 12 season just a week away from starting, this is our last chance to have a weekend off, a cue for Jodene and me to head away to the beach. You have to take all the opportunities you can because once the season starts there really isn't the chance to do anything like this at all.

Even then we have to be back early for fitness testing on Monday morning. We were actually tested at the end of the year before going on our Christmas break and then another one around the end of January to see how we were going. Sometimes skin fold tests are done but we don't do beep tests.

We did speed testing over 40 metres and our phosphate readings were also taken. With the speed test, we have just two chances to set a time and then a couple of days later we have to do a 3km time trial. I had a personal best of around 4.65s for the 40m so I was fairly pleased with that. You're supposed to be getting slower when you get older! It looks like I'm getting quicker, which I'm definitely not complaining about. My phosphate reading was also better than last year.

In the afternoon we had a compulsory team appearance at the Avondale races. We just put ourselves about on an occasion like that, have lunch with the sponsors and do some signing. It's something I find enjoyable.

While that reflects a reasonably typical week leading up to a new season, we move through to more team-oriented training as warm-up matches come onto the programme. And when the Super 12 season proper starts it all changes again.

If we're heading into a Friday night game, then on a Monday we'd probably start with a weights session in the morning and work on defence in the afternoon. By Tuesday we'd be looking at team work and trying to organise our game plan again while on Wednesday we'd probably have a day off. Come Thursday, we'd have a light run in the morning and then play Friday night. There'd always be a day off during the week. If we play Friday nights, we usually have the weekend off after it, which is quite good.

Whiteboard work becomes part of the drill here and there, probably mainly when we do our defence session. Graham Henry used to do that all the time when he was working with us on our defensive strategies. We do that sort of stuff early in the week to get it out of the way, concentrating on the opposition, and, as the week goes on, we worry more about ourselves and what we're trying to achieve.

When match days arrive, nothing's worse for players than night games. They really are a pain to prepare for because it's just a long time to wait around to play. I still haven't got used to the demands even though it's now very rare to have an afternoon match.

For home games, we assemble the night before at Sky City, have a team dinner and stay there. Most of the guys have a rub that night and get some physio. On the morning of the game we have breakfast together about 10.00 then jump on the bus and head off somewhere so we can get off and have a bit of a walk around and have a run through a few of our moves. After that, we normally find somewhere to have a cup of coffee, back at the hotel for lunch and then most of the guys will have an afternoon sleep. I quite like to have a doze but sometimes you just can't get to sleep.

The coach will have his meeting later in the day before we all get on the bus and head to the ground. We try to keep it as laid back as we can at that stage, aiming to arrive at the ground about an hour ahead of kick-off. There's no point being there any earlier.

Even though the game is professional and many things have changed not a lot is different about the final build-up for a match. About 35 minutes before kick-off we go out on to the ground or an adjoining ground if there is one to warm up for about 20-25 minutes before going back to the dressing room with about 10 minutes to go to put our boots on. That's still very much the same.

What has changed from some years back is the half-time break which used to be just a few minutes but is now 10 minutes. It was probably a bit strange at first having such a long half-time break but to be honest it doesn't usually feel like 10 minutes. By the time you get in the dressing room, sit down, have a drink and listen while the coach has a say, you're back out there again going through a couple of grids on the field. Obviously the length of the break suits television's commercial needs and there's no issue with that.

Once the game's over and we're showered and changed, we might have a function to attend, some sponsors to mingle with or we head out for a few quiets. The beer hasn't changed in all those years and the night after playing is always fair game for a few. The more some things change, the more they can stay the same. Sometimes.

But on balance the rugby world is so much different from the one I first knew on arriving in Auckland for the 1994 season. It was real old-style then, when footy training was always at night under some dodgy lights and you worked during the day. Because the game went professional fairly soon after that, I haven't really spent too much time working as such, apart from a bit of drain-laying back home and working for a printing company when I first came to Auckland. I don't miss it just quietly.

But I love this existence. It's awesome being able to have a working life built around training and playing rugby. I've never settled into a rhythm or routine on a weekly basis, rather just taking it day by day and there's not really one aspect of a pro's life that bothers me too much. Sure there's not always a lot of time to fit things in around training all the time but it's hardly a major issue. I wouldn't have it any other way... if only that form teacher could see me now.

www.franchise.co.nz

Franchise
New Zealand

The buy your own business magazine

Volume 13 Issue 1 Autumn 2004 $7.25

Carlos Spencer Scores a Franchise

Making The Right Decision

The Importance of Support

Funding Your Franchise

Re-Selling Your Business

Franchising's Forgotten Heroine

Long Black

Short Black

All Black

ESQUIRES
COFFEE HOUSES

Proudly supported by

Westpac

Endorsed by

Inside Westpac **Directory of Franchising**

CHAPTER 17

Los inc

BEFORE I KNOW IT, life won't be like this anymore. Give it just a few more years and there won't be constant training demands, there won't be test matches for the All Blacks, Super 12 games for the Blues or anything like that. It will no longer be a case of being paid a good salary to play rugby and to travel to various parts of the world.

I'm not sure I want to give too much serious thought to what that will be like exactly. When you've trained for so long and played so much rugby, the idea of suddenly not doing it will be a shock to the system. It's a time that comes to everyone who plays rugby for a living these days but I don't think it makes it any easier to adapt to because all of us have different ways of preparing for it and different ways of dealing with it.

My new contract with the New Zealand Rugby Union takes me to the end of 2006 and closer to that time I'll give my playing options due consideration although, if you asked me right now, I can't actually see myself going overseas to finish my playing career. I've had offers in the past and they still come in now but it's not the lifestyle I'd be interested in at that age, or could imagine myself being interested in then. I'd be doing it only for the money then if I was to go that way and I wouldn't enjoy that. I play this game because I love to be involved in it and I happen to be paid for it as well. That's the order it goes in and I'd hate to play just to be paid without enjoying it. I'd probably walk to the bank and smile at the money coming in but I can tell you going to training and playing probably would-

Summing up the way my life is moving. Soon rugby will be over so I've been looking at business opportunities, like Esquires Coffee Houses franchises.

n't make me smile that much at all.

If I was to do another year I suspect it would be here in New Zealand at this stage. Because my long-term playing future is so uncertain, I've been spending an increasing amount of time over the past few years – and especially in 2004 – considering my life outside rugby and beyond it. Suddenly it has begun to matter to me so, by the time I finish, I'll hopefully have a few businesses here to keep things ticking along. The business side of life has sparked me up a lot and I can't wait to be heavily involved.

A few years ago I told DOJ I was keen to get into landscape gardening and I still could be interested in that at some stage but right now there are other pursuits keeping me occupied. It's so healthy and refreshing to have something else to focus on as well. It's DOJ who keeps pumping ideas out that make me think and since Greg Dyer has been providing advice as well, he gives me even more to consider.

DOJ: *"Carlos is going to be lost without his rugby and that's why we needed to put some things in place. About five or six years ago he was thinking about landscape gardening as a possibility. That's changed as have a number of things in terms of his after-rugby goals. About three years ago I mentioned the possibility of creating a website. His response was: 'Why would I want a website?'*

"I told him: 'Because you're an international figure and if it goes the right way you can provide access for fans, create your own customer base, sell advertising and develop your own brand, even clothing, which may lead to things outside rugby'.

"That's how I got Carlos into computers as well. I knew he was computer-phobic and when I started planning the website, I thought about the idea of it having a web diary so he could post photographs and messages to it, in the process learning about computers. We also got him a 'tablet' (a computer on which an electronic pen can be used for input rather than a keyboard).

"One of my ideas in terms of the functionality of what was on the website was to have some interactivity. I asked my daughter and a lot of young kids what they would like to see on it and one of the big ones to come through was a message board. Greg Dyer was really good, too, because he has a web-based background and he could think of other design elements. It's helping Carlos to connect with the fans."

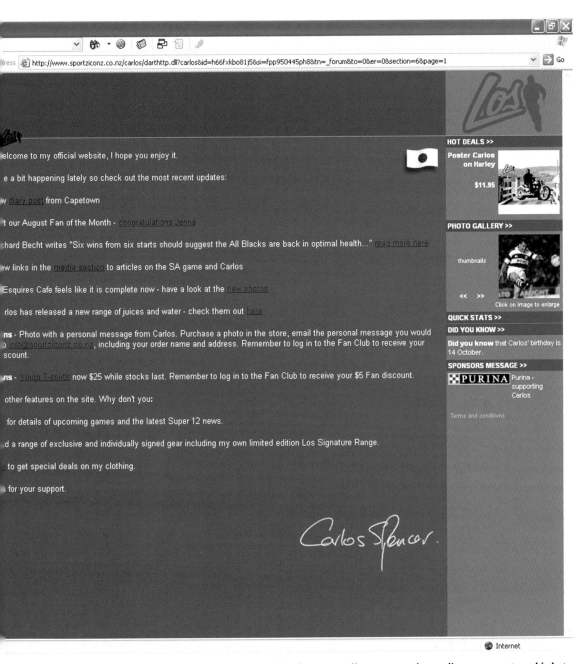

http://www.sportziconz.co.nz/carlos/darthttp.dll?carlos&id=h66fxkbo81j5&si=fpp950445ph8&tn=_forum&to=0&er=0&section=6&page=1

elcome to my official website, I hope you enjoy it.

e a bit happening lately so check out the most recent updates:

v diary post from Capetown

t our August Fan of the Month - congratulations Jenna

hard Becht writes "Six wins from six starts should suggest the All Blacks are back in optimal health..." read more here

w links in the media section to articles on the SA game and Carlos

Esquires Cafe feels like it is complete now - have a look at the new photos

rlos has released a new range of juices and water - check them out here

ns - Photo with a personal message from Carlos. Purchase a photo in the store, email the personal message you would
) info@sportziconz.co.nz, including your order name and address. Remember to log in to the Fan Club to receive your
scount.

ns - Youth T-shirts now $25 while stocks last. Remember to log in to the Fan Club to receive your $5 Fan discount.

other features on the site. Why don't you:

for details of upcoming games and the latest Super 12 news.

d a range of exclusive and individually signed gear including my own limited edition Los Signature Range.

to get special deals on my clothing.

for your support.

HOT DEALS >>
Poster Carlos on Harley
$11.95

PHOTO GALLERY >>
thumbnails
<< >>
Click on image to enlarge

QUICK STATS >>
DID YOU KNOW >>
Did you know that Carlos' birthday is 14 October.

SPONSORS MESSAGE >>
PURINA Purina - supporting Carlos

Terms and conditions

Internet

My website www.carlosspencer.co.nz has been a totally new experience. I'm no computer whiz but I'm having fun with it.

Setting up the website has opened a new world to me. I lacked confidence when it came to even thinking about computers but now it's a point of special interest. I'm not the best in the world but I'm not afraid of computers now. That's been good for me and it's something I really like. For me the computer has been a toy in many ways because I never really used one before so I've been flat out

My favourite number and one of my favourite tattoos promote the website where we market merchandise under the Los brand.

learning all about it. I'm not too big on searching for too many sites, unless they're ones to do with motorbikes. As well as that I look at messages on the message board on my site and send out replies. Most of the guys are fairly computer-savvy now. Computer classes have been run over the years to help out.

Heaps of messages are coming in on my website and I'm not too bad at responding to a lot of them. Obviously I don't have time to do the whole lot but I make an effort. Every now and then I end up having a conversation online with someone. I might yarn with someone for a few minutes. I feel good about it and I hope it's helping the fans as well. I suppose it helps to make you more accessible and more human in a way. The reason why I got involved in having a site was to do it for the fans, to give them something back for their support and to let them know what I'm doing outside training.

It was DOJ's idea to do this and he did the same for Dougy (Howlett). I wasn't that keen at first. I didn't think I needed to be doing something like this. What do I want a website for? Then I thought about the fans and there was also DOJ's idea of coming up with my own range of "Los" merchandise – based on my nickname – and selling it online. It all stacked up well. Why not give it a go? I've been happy with it.

There's a lot of traffic on the message board, not always to do with me. Quite often there are just conversations going on between people talking about all sorts of things but I try to put something up there as regularly as I can. So when we were in camp in Palmerston North preparing for the 2004 All Black trial, I put this out on the message board:

> *"Been in camp for three days now, the weather has decided to pack in this afternoon after a couple of days of sunshine. Trainings haven't been too hard, just a lot of organising at the moment so everyone can come to grips with the game plan. Been having a couple of sessions a day. The team are out for dinner tonight at the Lone Star in PaImy, so I'm looking forward to a big steak. Hope everyone's well. Take it easy and I'll catch ya later. Cheers Los!!!"*

It's all about that sort of connection. It's not a business venture but more, as DOJ says, a case of me being seen as accessible to supporters and developing my brand for outside rugby. The big business investment for me recently has come through the Esquires Coffee Houses franchise we bought in Auckland. A lot of work went into that project.

> **DOJ:** *"Carlos said at one stage that he wouldn't mind having a coffee bar and he also mentioned a juice bar. He said he wanted to get into a restaurant, too, and that's when I got Greg Dyer in to look at a few things for him. Carlos was thinking about things, which was really good, but he's sensible enough not to rush and to take advice. He has the impulse that he wants to do something but he knows it has to make sense. Jodene's been good for him in that sense as well, in helping him to think about opportunities outside and after rugby.*
> *"If you can start something up that's running parallel to your rugby career, which Carlos is with the Esquires Coffee Houses venture, I think it actually makes you a better player because you have other interests."*

With the Esquires enterprise, the plan is to have perhaps three franchises up and running in the near future and maybe after that I might branch out into some other areas. The Esquires venture also brought about some rather different publicity. I was used on a magazine cover with a rugby flavour, only it wasn't for a rugby magazine. It was *Franchise* playing up my involvement in the Esquires chain.

Marketing and advertising opportunities come along as well although they're not things we chase too aggressively. They tend to come as a result of approaches made to us. I guess the one that stands out for most people was the work I did with Toffee Pops. It's a money issue when those opportunities come along and

Whether it's a long black, flat white or latté, I'm onto it now after buying into the Esquires Coffee Houses chain.

you make it while you can. I certainly had that Toffee Pops image for a few years. It was hard to shake off and maybe I still haven't.

In 2004, I also had a marketing outlet when the pet food company Purina, featured me in a promotion encouraging people to look after their dogs' health. Purina obviously found out I was a dog owner, possibly through shots I had on my website of Sarj and Diesel. They approached an agent who then contacted me to see whether I'd be interested. I loved that opportunity to involve the dogs.

I've had some smaller things to do as well for a bit of extra money. I've also done a couple of stories with local magazines. Jodene and I did a spread with our son Payton for *Woman's Day* but I've also turned away a lot of approaches from magazines because I haven't really been interested in what they wanted to do.

Of all the things I've done outside rugby, I guess the Toffee Pops image is one that's stuck the longest.

The website offers merchandising opportunities selling Los brand caps and shirts while we also market the Los rugby ball, Los juice and Los water. I'm involved in signing memorabilia and we've had a major breakthrough with the NZRU – they've given me permission to market my regular playing number – 10 – on the All Black strip, the first time any player has been allowed to do that.

Another area a lot of All Blacks head into when they retire is media and commentary work as well as the public speaking circuit. I can't imagine Carlos Spencer doing the speaking circuit. In fact, put money on that because it's not my scene at all. I'm not a very talkative person at the best of times, certainly not in front of a crowd. But never say never!

There's a lot of action going on outside actually training for and playing rugby. It's positive, though, and I find it so exciting. My outlook on life has changed and I feel a lot more comfortable about what I'll be doing when I finish playing. I know when I'm around the guys, I often find myself talking to them about business plans and business opportunities. I'm sure "bottom line" has been dropped into the discussion from time to time. There's no way I would have been talking about subjects even close to business a few years back. Then it would have been strictly boy's stuff.

One thing I do know now is that I'm prepared for life after rugby and that's more than I could say not that long ago.

This was one of my favourite ventures. Pet food company Purina approached me about a promotion to encourage people to look after their dogs' health. I love my dogs Sarj and Diesel so I couldn't resist this one.

CHAPTER 18

Hi Dad

RUGBY RULES JUST ABOUT EVERYTHING I DO and almost always wins as well. Nothing much gets in the way of the way it impacts on my life. I know even when I stop playing, it will still be having a strong say in some way. But in early part of the 2004 season, rugby wasn't always the winner. There was an event that wasn't going to make way for my job or anything else for that matter. This was one that would essentially happen in its own good time. Sure there was a little bit of pressure and some encouragement to fit it into a certain window but this was nature taking its course and it wasn't going to be dictated to by a bloke named Carlos Spencer and the rugby commitments he had on his plate.

Yes, in years to come Payton Cruz Spencer will be able to tell everyone he had a mind of his own in April 2004 and he wasn't at all concerned whether his dad was supposed to be somewhere playing a game of rugby.

That's jumping a little bit ahead, though. Let me first back up a long, long way back to my Horowhenua days when I was a shy kid out of Levin, as distinct from a shy bloke from Auckland. I was brought up well in normal surroundings with my brother Fabian. I finished up going to a fairly standard secondary school in Waiopehu College. I only really knew of Jo through my girlfriend at the time, who was in Jo's netball team.

Nothing changes life like having your own children and having Payton in our lives has made a huge difference.

"We knew each other vaguely through high school but only from a distance and not to walk up and say hello. We were from opposite ends of the pole really. I was at a girls' school – Palmerston North Girls' High School – and he was at Waiopehu College and we saw each other only through occasional athletics meets and the odd netball game. There was nothing more to it than that."

After knowing of each other as teenagers I headed to Auckland and Jodene went her own way. There was every chance we might never have seen each other again I suppose. To be honest I don't think either one of us gave it much more thought than that.

"But then out of the blue we saw each other at an All Black after-match function. Carlos wasn't single nor was I but we met and he put out his hand to say: 'Hi, I'm...' Before he could say anything else I said: 'Yes, I know who you are'.
"I moved to Sydney for 10 months after that, he carried on doing his thing and when I returned home we had a chance meeting in town and it just went from there.
"It happened so fast. We went out for lunch, which turned into dinner and that was it. We were fairly much together from then on in. We'd moved in together only about six weeks after I'd met him, in the first house he owned in St Johns. He was very proud of that house and it was a lovely home."

We're talking late 1998 here, and no one needs reminding that '98 wasn't a good year at all for the All Blacks just a year out from the Rugby World Cup in the Northern Hemisphere. I was well-established in Auckland by then, having just completed my fifth season since moving from Levin and I'd also had a taste of being an All Black as well. Obviously 1999 was an even more critical year when the pressure was on everyone involved with the All Blacks, which meant Jodene and I wouldn't be seeing much of each other.

"I soon had to become used to being a rugby player's partner with all that time when Los is away. While he had a couple of years where he wasn't really part of the All Blacks, it didn't make that much difference because there was always something happening to do with rugby. Each Super 12 season is really demanding.
"I try to be as much of a support for him as I can be. As the years have gone by I think my knowledge of the game has improved and I tend to become a bit of a critic as well, listening to and learning a lot from Carlos' dad after sitting next to him for quite a few games. I have to remind myself, though, that I haven't been at that level and mentally I wouldn't know what Carlos goes through but I just try to be there and, if he wants to talk he does, if he doesn't want to then he doesn't. He's completely different off the field to what he is on it. When he's playing, he's an

extrovert. When he's not, he doesn't have anywhere near as much to say but there's still a lot of cheek there. He loves taking the mickey out of everyone he knows. He's caught me out a few times."

There's no doubt I've needed moral support at various times. I like to feel I'm in control and that I can handle bad situations. I also have a policy of not letting anything get me down, well, not for too long in any case. But I wouldn't be human if I didn't admit I have felt things sometimes even if I haven't shown it. Jo knows that.

"You read some of the comments in the media about Los and, while he doesn't seem to take them personally, I feel gutted for him. You offer support as much as you can both in his recovery from injuries and at selection times as well.

"One time he didn't make the All Blacks was the tour to Ireland, Scotland and Argentina in 2001. He didn't listen to that team being named but I did. He'd had such a great NPC that year yet he missed the side. He fought that one for a few days but generally he gets over them fairly quickly. He tends to stay close around times like that.

"The knee injury (in 1999) was bad. That was tough for both of us. I took time out from my studies because he was literally bed-ridden for the first 10 days or so after his operation."

After we'd been together for more than four years we decided to have a break from each other early in 2003, basically to test our relationship I guess.

It was only when we were apart that I realised how much Jo meant to me so one night I invited her for a home-cooked dinner and proposed to her. I knew then how much I wanted to be with Jo and in no time we were talking about much more than just being engaged.

"Within weeks of becoming engaged, we started talking about having children. Initially I wanted to do it the right way as such, to get married first and then have children but after becoming engaged the timing just seemed right. It felt like the right thing to do."

My original thought was that I wanted to wait until I'd finished playing rugby, or at least finished at international level, before starting a family. The more I thought about it, though, the less that mattered. We could still mix having a family while I kept playing rugby and, only three months later, Jodene was pregnant. Well, she told me she was but I took some convincing.

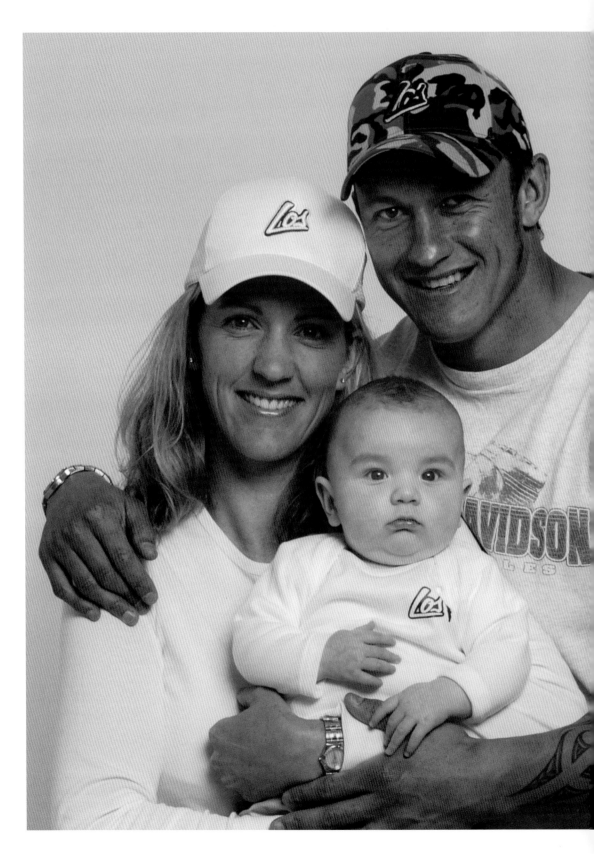

"It took Carlos a while to believe it was real. He didn't believe the pregnancy tests and he didn't believe the blood tests. He only believed it when I had a six and a half week scan. He realised it then. He's quite visual, wanting to see everything and have it right there and then. Because I didn't show for a long, long time it was like there was nothing going on. For the first four months or so of being pregnant I didn't really have much to do with Carlos because of the World Cup. In fact, the first time he saw me when I was really showing was a couple of weeks into the World Cup and it blew him away."

When I saw the scan, well, that was incredible. It certainly helped to be able to see there was something happening. I always like to be able to see things, especially this because it was all so new to me. I was buzzing after that but the trouble was I had to wait and I really wanted the baby straightaway. I always want everything right now, or maybe tomorrow, but I don't like waiting.

"I wanted to find out whether we were having a boy or a girl but Carlos didn't. He said to me: 'How many good surprises do we get in life? Let's just wait for this one'. He was absolutely right, although I think we would find out for the next one."

The big issue was the impact rugby would have on everything. Obviously I had off-season training to worry about and then the 2004 Super 12 season started. That meant I couldn't always be around to help and I missed out on a lot while Jo kept working right through until fairly late in the piece.

That was in February and, not long after, my rugby season received a bit of a setback when I had my jaw broken during the Blues' upset loss to the Chiefs.

The three of us . . . if rugby tended to come first before, family has taken over now.

*"It was a bonus in a way to have Los around then because it was obvious that try-
ing to organise the birth itself was going to be quite something. The due date was
May 4 at one point, then it came forward to April 27 and then it went forward
again. In the end we had a two-week window when we thought our baby would
come.
"Still, it was a nightmare trying to sort out where the birth would fit in around the
Super 12 programme. We got a bit uptight about sorting out the timing. Carlos just
wanted a date so plans could be made. He said: 'We need to have a day'. I said:
'Well, we do have a day but babies come when they're ready and there's not a lot
we can do about it'."*

We knew we would be clear for the match against the Bulls. That was never
likely to be a problem. The next week we were still at home, back at Eden Park
to take on the Stormers – let's not talk about that night too much – and then we
knew we were getting close, trying to figure out the options.

After that match, the Blues were looking at two matches in South Africa, the
first against the Cats in Johannesburg on April 24 and the second a week later
against the Sharks in Durban. So, now we were really wondering how things
would play out. We'd been to see our specialist about inducing Jodene and the
decision was made to go in on April 21, a Wednesday.

*"The Blues were super supportive, but I think ideally they would have liked Carlos
to be in South Africa in time so he could at least be on the bench for that first match.
If I'd had Payton, say, on Wednesday, Los probably would have flown out on
Thursday afternoon and he would have been there in time. That may have been plan
A but Payton had other ideas."*

There was no reason for nerves, even though this was all new for us. Our spe-
cialists gave us every confidence that everything would turn out fine. I was just so
excited. That's what I remember most about it all, that feeling of excitement. It
was a long wait, though, after going into National Women's Hospital on the
Wednesday night.

*"I know you don't win any brownie points when you're giving birth. Without
wanting to sound like a martyr, I wanted to be aware of the experience and I wanted to be quite mobile but that didn't happen. I had an epidural and that eased a lot
of the pain.
"By 4.00 on Thursday afternoon I was in established labour and Payton was born
at 12.25 on Friday morning (April 23). I watched Carlos the whole time. When
Payton came out I just saw this huge grin on Carlos' face. I knew then that we'd*

had a little boy. He just didn't stop grinning."

I couldn't wait for it all to happen. In the end I was just that overwhelmed, that happy and that proud seeing it all happen. As soon as the baby popped out I knew we had a son. I couldn't miss the giveaway sign and then to be able to cut Payton's cord as well – just awesome. I've heard so many people talking about seeing their children born and it was just magic, pure magic.

"Deep down I knew Carlos wanted a little boy first. I was so excited and so ready for Payton to be born. The labour itself was easily the hardest thing I've ever done but everything was still great and went really well with no complications. I can honestly say that two days after that I said I could go back and do it again."

Friday, April 23, 2004 – it was a blur at the time but it will always be one of the very best days in my life, the day I became a dad. I had so many people to tell about it. Within half an hour, I started sending texts out and Mum and Dad headed up from Levin as soon as they could, knowing they'd become grandparents for the third time. They drove up that day and it was so good that I was able to be there with them when Jo and I could show them Payton. It made me feel proud, them, too. It was just a great day in every way.

By 3.00 that morning we had already moved from the hospital to Birthcare in Parnell. Jo was really well looked after in there. At least I had a bit of time with her and Payton but somehow I had to switch my mind back to rugby at some point. I have to admit that wasn't easy. I was meant to go on April 24 – the Saturday – but I rang up our manager (Ant Strachan) and asked whether I could have one more day at home before flying to South Africa. I was really glad they said yes.

Even better, I left on Sunday knowing the boys had beaten the Cats and secured maximum points. We went on to do the same to the Sharks the following weekend but I know I was thinking a lot about Jodene and Payton back home. It's a completely different feeling when you're away from home for the first time after becoming a father. You just wish you could be at home.

Whenever we arrive home from overseas, I'm normally a bit slow getting my bags and coming through customs but this time I was the first out, rushing through because Jodene was there with Payton. I was so glad to be back and in no time we were on our way home.

"That was a tough week for us. Our phone bills are always massive when Carlos is away. He's always calling home and he was certainly on the phone a lot that week.

"You have to be a certain type of character to be a rugby partner. You have to be independent and to learn to get on with things. If you sit at home pining for them it won't do you or them any good. I've pretty much had Payton to myself which I think Carlos has found tough. It's difficult for a father to bond with a newborn baby because all they really need is their mum. He makes up for it doing everything he can. I expressed milk so Carlos had the chance to feed Payton which was really important. He went from an extremely cruisy man to getting impatient when Payton cried because he couldn't fix it. He didn't know what to do, how to calm this baby.
"The nicest thing of all, though, is seeing Payton with his Daddy and the look on Los' face whenever he has him. I took him into the Heritage to see Carlos when the All Blacks were in camp after the team had been named in June. Kees, Doug (Howlett), Sammy (Tuitupou), Joe (Rokocoko) and some of the others came over to have a cuddle and Los had that 'that's my boy' look all over his face.
"You think you love someone as much as you can and then you see them with their children and you love them even more."

Having Payton has put a whole new perspective on life. Now there's much more to it than just rugby which before was fairly much No 1. Suddenly family definitely comes first.

We've talked about having more children and we certainly plan to. That's still ahead of us. We also have our wedding to worry about in January 2005 so there's plenty to think about. For now, I love the chance to come home to see Payton and do whatever I can, to have my turn giving him a bath, changing him and feeding him. It's all just so good.

Because of my rugby I haven't been able to help as much as I'd like. I was able to go to only a couple of ante-natal classes so Jo's had a bit of a time of it really. She's been great because so much of the work she's had to do on her own.

"This is a huge change for Carlos, for me and for us but he was ready for this. He has matured a lot over the last few years. I think he's definitely considering the future more since Payton was born. We're thinking of having two more but we can't be sure where life will take us. We don't know where rugby is going to go."

By the time Payton was six weeks old – and stacking on the weight, let me say – we wanted everyone to have the chance to see the reason for our happiness by doing a feature and photo shoot for *Woman's Day*. That in turn created a fair bit of traffic on the message board on my website...

Happiness is a father with his baby son . . . one of the photos in the feature Jo and I did with *Woman's Day* when Payton was six weeks old.

The *Woman's Day* spread gave everyone the chance to see the reason for our joy – Payton Cruz with his mum and dad.

2004-05-31 11:49:15

the pics of Payton Cruz Spencer are just gorgeous! and its a great article to read too. Los sounds like a very relaxed and a helpful dad in the article, which is lovely. and they are planning a huge wedding next january. All the best Los for the wedding and helping little Payton grow up to be as great as you! love and hugs Liv xxx

2004-05-31 12:34:00

Yes yes i read that, that is awesome aint it, well ive just gotten back from getting a copy and i read it and thought it was kewl, and the wedding wow, hope cuzzin rico is going ill give him my digi cam so he can take some pics, and send them to me..hehe…he probably take his own cam(lol).

But great as it is to be a dad, some things never change. I still have my job to do. There are games to be played, training sessions to do, game plans to think about as my rugby world keeps going. I can't forget about it because it's my livelihood. My passion for rugby hasn't diminished but there's a new dimension to my life. Jodene's been a part of it for close to six years but there's a totally different emphasis now Payton Cruz has become the No 1 attraction. And he really is No 1 in our home now. Sorry about that Jo, Sarj and Diesel.

Once Payton had joined us, though, I had to stay tuned to rugby needs. At first that was finishing off Super 12 business with the Blues, which hardly ended the way we wanted but it was still a big improvement on what we were looking at after five or so weeks.

I'd be lying if I didn't admit the big attraction of the rugby year was retaining my job in the All Blacks' No 10 jersey and not just for that reason alone. I wouldn't have minded if John Mitchell had still been coach, or if someone else – anyone else – had the job for that matter but I'm honest enough to say the prospect of being in the All Blacks with Graham Henry as coach was just that little bit special.

I also knew, though, that there wouldn't be a walk-up start. Everything begins all over again when a new coach comes into the position. He brings in new selectors and new ideas which makes it a nervous time for those who have been All Blacks recently. You can't help wondering where you fit into their plans, or whether you fit in at all actually.

As I always say, Ted has been a huge influence on my rugby career and on my life, too. I owe him plenty but I still had to prove I deserved a place in his team.

For the first time in years, we had an All Black trial and it didn't run as smoothly for me personally as I would have liked. But the next day I was as thrilled as I've ever been to discover I was in Ted's first All Black team. That meant a lot to me when I think back to him encouraging me to come to Auckland in 1994 and now, all those years later, he was going to be my All Black coach. There was something else that couldn't be missed. When I first made the All Blacks in 1995, I did so as a replacement for Andrew Mehrtens. Here we were nine years later and Mehrts was making a comeback from the wilderness to return to the All Blacks. Talk about some things never changing!

I'll admit it made a big difference to me personally playing my first test with Ted as my All Black coach on a very chilly June night at Carisbrook in Dunedin. The occasion was my 30th test overall with the world champions England our opponents and it still takes some believing now that the score finished 36-3 in our favour. It has to rank as one of the best tests I've been involved in. I don't think anyone could have imagined we would win by 33 points, not even in the team. It was a heck of a start to the season, especially for a new All Black team and a new set of coaches.

In what was my fifth test against England, everything about it just went so well, before in the lead-up and then during the full 80 minutes. It took us a while to come to grips with the game plan the coaches wanted us to play but it certainly seemed to work out on the night in one of those performances when everyone did their job and did it well. And, of course, it all started up front where it should. This time we were right on form in every respect. It was amazing to see how much things could change in the space of seven months since the 2003 World Cup dream ended.

For me it was the start of another phase of my rugby career, being exposed to my fifth different All Black coach in nine years. This one was a lot different, too. I knew I was playing for another person and a very important one. I thought about Payton in the lead-up to the match but I'd have to say there was just a bit too much going on during the game to stop to think about him.

When the test was over, my mind was soon thinking about getting back home knowing there was a little one waiting for me. It really gives you something to look forward to but, by the time Payton was seven weeks old, rugby had already robbed me of a lot of time seeing him. I'd probably been around for no more than two weeks, maybe three tops. It's difficult and then, when I do get home, he's usually asleep so I can't see much of him. I miss the little fella and it's hard on Jo doing everything with me being away so much. I'm always trying to find some excuse to get him up so I can hold him, making a bit of noise here and there.

What I've noticed above all is that Payton makes me feel more at ease when I'm preparing for a match. I've always made a big effort to try to relax and get away from rugby as much as possible leading up to a game and now that's much easier because he takes my mind off it. It helps to keep your mind fresh when you don't have to think about rugby all the time and he does that automatically. I'm no longer just Carlos Spencer, rugby player. Now I'm Carlos Spencer, dad — and I love that bit.

CARLOS SPENCER

FIRST CLASS CAREER STATISTICS

(TO END OF TRI NATIONS CUP 2004)

Team	Period	Games	Tries	Conv	Pens	Drops	Points
Auckland	94–02	84	38	71	43	6	479
New Zealand	95–04	44	16	72	53		383
New Zealand A	1999	4	1	12	11	1	65
Horowhenua	92–93	18	11	35	23		192
NZ Trials	97–04	3					
NZ Colts	94–95	5	2	4	5		33
Colts Trial	1995	1		1	3		11
NZ Maori	94–02	9	4	11	3	1	54
North Island	1995	1	2				10
NZ Barbarians	1996	1	1	1	2		13
UK Barbarians	2001	1					
Blues	96–04	91	24	120	78	3	603
Total		262	99	327	221	11	1843

- All Black number 951
- In the last match of the All Black tour to the UK at the end of 1997 he became just the fourth All Black to score 200 points in a calendar year. He scored 202 points – those before him were Grant Fox 1987: Don Clarke 1960: Billy Wallace 1905.
- The 33 points he scored in his debut test match against Argentina was then the second highest debut score; and the then second highest All Black test match score – both to Simon Culhane. It was then the fourth highest score by any player in a test match.
- Shares with Simon Culhane and Andrew Mehrtens the record of achieving 100 points in their first five tests.
- The 25 points he scored at Eden Park in 1997 was then the second highest scored by anyone in a test match against South Africa.
- He scored five tries for Auckland against Otago in the 1996 NPC semi-final.
- His test matches have been against – Australia 10, South Africa 7, England 6, France 3, Argentina 2, Italy 2, Wales 2, Canada 1, Pacific Islands 1, Tonga 1.
- His test match tries have been scored against – Argentina 3, Italy 3, South Africa 3, England 2, Wales 2, Tonga 1.
- His 14 test match tries are the most by an All Black first five-eighth.
- Has represented New Zealand Under 16 Softball in 1990-91.

SUPER 12 TRIES – Hurricanes 3, Crusaders 3, Natal 3, Highlanders 2, Brumbies 2, Reds 2, Bulls 2, Northern Transvaal 2, Stormers 2, Waratahs 1, Gauteng Lions 1, Western Province 1.